The Economic Theory of Professional Team Sports

NEW HORIZONS IN THE ECONOMICS OF SPORT

Series Editors: Wladimir Andreff, *Department of Economics, University of Paris 1 Panthéon Sorbonne, France* and Marc Lavoie, *Department of Economics, University of Ottawa, Canada*

For decades, the economics of sport was regarded as a hobby for a handful of professional economists who were primarily involved in other areas of research. In recent years, however, the significance of the sports economy as a percentage of GDP has expanded dramatically. This has coincided with an equivalent rise in the volume of economic literature devoted to the study of sport.

This series provides a vehicle for deeper analyses of the demand for sport, cost–benefit analysis of sport, sporting governance, the economics of professional sports and leagues, individual sports, trade in the sporting goods industry, media coverage, sponsoring and numerous related issues. It will contribute to the further development of sports economics by welcoming new approaches and highlighting original research in both established and newly emerging sporting activities. The series aims to publish the best theoretical and empirical work from well-established researchers and academics, as well as from talented newcomers in the field.

Titles in the series include:

The Economics of Sport and the Media
Edited by Claude Jeanrenaud and Stefan Késenne

The Economic Theory of Professional Team Sports
An Analytical Treatment
Stefan Késenne

The Economic Theory of Professional Team Sports

An Analytical Treatment

Stefan Késenne

Professor of Economics, University of Antwerp and Catholic University of Leuven, Belgium

NEW HORIZONS IN THE ECONOMICS OF SPORT

Edward Elgar
Cheltenham, UK • Northampton, MA, USA

Published by
Edward Elgar Publishing Limited
Glensanda House
Montpellier Parade
Cheltenham
Glos GL50 1UA
UK

Edward Elgar Publishing, Inc.
William Pratt House
9 Dewey Court
Northampton
Massachusetts 01060
USA

A catalogue record for this book
is available from the British Library

Library of Congress Cataloguing in Publication Data

Késenne, Stefan.
  The economic theory of professional team sports : an analytical treatment / by Stefan Késenne.
    p. cm. — (New horizons in the economics of sport series)
  Includes bibliographical references and index.
  1. Sports teams—Economic aspects. 2. Professional sports—Economic aspects. I. Title.

GV716.K47 2007
796.06′91—dc22   2007010626

ISBN 978 1 84720 207 9 (cased)

Printed and bound in Great Britain by MPG Books Ltd, Bodmin, Cornwall

Contents

Contents   vii

Figures

Tables

Symbols

A	attendance
AC	average cost
AR	average revenue
C	total cost
c	unit cost of talent
c^0	fixed capital cost
cap	salary cap
D	demand
E	equilibrium
e	effort
ε	elasticity
g_w	expected number of wins
k	proportionality factor
L	total number of players in a team
l	number of players
m	market size
MC	marginal cost
MR	marginal revenue
μ	share parameter
n	number of clubs in a league
NAR	net average revenue
p	price
π	profit
Q	quality
q	quantity
R	revenue
RME	rate of monopsonistic exploitation
s	supply
σ	win bonus
t	talent
τ	tax rate
TV	television
u	utility
uo	uncertainty of outcome

v	fund
w	season winning percentage
x	large-market team
y	small-market team

Foreword

The main objective of this book is to put at my students' disposal a text with a more rigorous and analytical treatment of the theory of professional team sports than is presently on offer. My class on sports economics at the University of Antwerp is taught to undergraduate students in applied economics.

The book concentrates on professional team sports only. It is not a textbook on sports economics, nor a textbook on the economics of team sports because it does not deal with recreational team sports. The distinction between the professional and recreational sports industries is important because, from an economic point of view, they constitute two different worlds. In professional team sports, the consumer is the spectator who is willing to pay to watch the players playing their games at a stadium or on television. The producer is the club or the league and the production output is the game or the league championship. The main factor of production is the player, playing is work and the player is paid for his or her performances. In recreational team sports, the consumer is the player or the sports participant who is willing to pay for his or her club membership. Playing is consumption. The production output is the service offered by the sports club to the sports participant. In professional team sports, watching sport is the focus of interest whereas in recreational sports it is practising sport. It goes without saying that an economic analysis of both sports sectors will be fundamentally different.

It is not the ambition of this textbook to be complete, even within the relatively small field of the economic theory of professional team sports. Given that the emphasis is on theory and analysis, little attention is paid to institutions and structural differences between the sports industries in North America, Europe and Australia. Many institutional differences do not touch the basic relationships if the theory is kept on a highly abstract level. Only to the extent that the sports structures do affect the basic hypotheses and dominant relationships of the model will they be addressed. Apart from the most basic and robust empirical results, which are helpful in specifying the models, empirical applications and verifications of the theory are also left out. Moreover, in order to stay within the planned volume of this book, many important and interesting topics in sports economics are not covered because a selection had to be made. Also, in some areas, the literature did not offer a clear theoretical and analytical framework while in others the mathematical treatment was too advanced for undergraduate students. To make the theoretical analysis more accessible, simplifying the specifications of some relationships were necessary.

Nevertheless, I hope that this textbook fills a gap in the growing market of books on sports economics by providing an analytical approach to the theory of professional team sports. I wish to thank all my colleagues, in particular the many sports economists from Europe and North America who have become good friends. The many discussions I have had with them during international conferences and meetings have been a great help in writing this book.

Finally, for the sake of readability, this book has been framed throughout in the masculine gender. This is in no way intended to exclude or denigrate the role of female sports participants.

1. The peculiar economics of professional team sports

1.1 INTRODUCTION

The economics of professional team sports is a young and relatively small field of academic research. Simon Rottenberg, an economist at the University of Massachusetts at Amherst, is generally considered to be the pioneer of sports economics with his seminal article on the baseball player market, published in the *Journal of Political Economy* in 1956. After 50 years, and notwithstanding a rapid growth in the number of sports papers over the last decades, Rottenberg's article still looks remarkably up-to-date, and is a must on every reading list for students of sports economics. Another pioneer in the short history of economic thought on team sports is Walter Neale, with his paper *The peculiar economics of professional sports*, published in the *Quarterly Journal of Economics* in 1964. Surprisingly enough, neither economist published any other significant contribution to the field. In the late sixties and early seventies, other economists took over and continued to publish regularly on the subject: James Quirk, Gerald Scully and Roger Noll in the USA; Colin Jones in Canada; Peter Sloane in the UK; and Braham Dabscheck in Australia. A milestone in economic research on professional team sports was a book edited by Roger Noll (1974c), *Government and the Sports Business*. This collection of excellent papers, presented at probably the first ever conference on sports economics, has inspired a growing number of economists to concentrate on team sports. To the best of our knowledge, *Pay Dirt*, written by James Quirk and Rodney Fort (1992), and *Baseball and Billions*, written by Andrew Zimbalist (1992) are the first monographs on sports economics (although the doctoral dissertation of H.G. Demmert (1973), *The Economics of Professional Team Sports*, is often overlooked as an important early contribution to the theory).

At the turn of the century, The International Association of Sports Economists (IASE) was founded in France and a new journal was started in California, called *The Journal of Sports Economics*, which mainly publishes studies and papers on professional team sports. Since then, a growing number of sports conferences have been organised and new books and conference proceedings have been published so that, gradually, sports economics has become a fully developed field of research. A two-volume book, edited by Andrew Zimbalist (2001) presents an excellent collection of papers written between 1950 and 2000. Wladimir Andreff and Stefan Szymanski (2006) edited a book with 86 contributions covering all important topics in sports economics written by 65 prominent sports economists.

1.2   PECULIARITIES

When a new field of research takes off, the first question asked is whether there is any justification for devoting a separate field of economic research to it. This applies equally to professional team sports. Is there anything special or exceptional about the industry? Neale (1964) pointed to the most important economic characteristics that make the industry of professional team sports different from other industries. He called it the inverted joint product. Economists are familiar with 'joint products': one single production process yields two or more different products. 'Inverted joint product' refers to a situation where two production processes by two companies are needed to produce and supply one single product. In team sports, the companies are the sports clubs, the product is the game. One team cannot play a football match – it needs an opponent team. If the product is not just one individual game but also the league championship, more than two clubs are necessary.

Moreover, sport is basically about competition. If the playing strengths of two teams are too far apart so that one team always wins without much competition, the product is not very interesting for people to watch. So, a second peculiar characteristic of the industry is that a certain degree of competitive balance between the teams is necessary in order to sell the product. Sports lose its attractiveness if there isn't any uncertainty of outcome in a championship. Although there is some disagreement among sports economists about the optimal degree of competitive balance (see Szymanski, 2003), it cannot be denied that a minimum of outcome uncertainty is necessary. To watch a football team winning by 12 goals to 1 can be great fun once, but no real sports fan wants to experience the same huge score in each game, week after week.

These two characteristics of the team sports industry have had serious consequences for the competition policy on product and labour markets. If more clubs are involved in supplying the product, such as a league championship, some cooperation between the clubs is necessary. It is obvious that a well-organised championship is more interesting to watch than a number of occasional individual games. So, some regulation of the product market is called for. How many clubs can enter the product market, and under what conditions? How many times is the product to be supplied to the public, and which clubs will meet when and where? So, club owners came together and created a union, a federation or a league, which is, in economic terms, a cartel of clubs. If more than one league was created covering a specific area, they merged after some time, so that, in most sport disciplines, a monopoly league became the rule. Economists, however, cherish competition and competitive markets, and are opposed to cartels and monopolies because they cause welfare losses by charging prices that are too high and production outputs that are too low. Given the existing antitrust legislation, the question is whether the team sports industry is entitled to an antitrust exemption. Whereas the business strategy of firms in most sectors of the economy is to get rid of fierce competitors in order to build a strong and comfortable market position, the same strategy in the sports industry would kill the business because a sports team needs opponents of more-or-less equal strength.

Also, competition on the player labour market has come under fire. Without free entry to the product market and free relocation of teams, it is argued that a free player market threatens the competitive balance in the league because the rich clubs in the large city markets can hire all the best players by offering the highest salaries. So, a free player labour market would destroy the sports business. Moreover, the hiring of playing talent by a team can create a negative external effect. Club owners do not always realise and take account of the fact that strengthening their own teams weakens the opponent teams in the league.

Neale (1964) concluded from these considerations that the team sports industry shows some characteristics of a natural monopoly. He also claimed that the league, and not the club, should be the single production entity and the employer of the players, so that the league can allocate the players to the clubs, as the league's local branches, in order to guarantee the necessary uncertainty of outcome. Most sports economists, however, as well as many jurists (see Ross, 1991) disagree. Even if they accept that a monopoly league is not necessarily anticompetitive, they do not approve of the creation of a local monopoly position for each club, the strict limitation of the number of teams in the top league, the restrictions to the freedom of players to move to other teams, the pooling of television rights by the league and so on (see Noll, 1999). In most professional team sports, the clubs are largely independent entities and the employers of the players, but the sports league tries to control and regulate the product and player market. The most common market regulations are restrictions on player mobility by creating a so-called reservation system or retain and transfer system. There are also different arrangements to share revenues among clubs, and leagues impose salary or payroll caps. These corrections to the free market outcomes aim to improve the attractiveness of the games, by guaranteeing a reasonable competitive balance in the league, and to hold down top players' salaries.

Given the peculiarities of the professional team sports industry, many interesting questions can be raised. Is the objective of profit maximisation described in classical microeconomics textbooks also what sports clubs are aiming at? Or is a club owner more interested in winning, and what are the implications? How has the growing impact of globalisation and broadcasting changed the industry? Do we need restrictions on player mobility to improve competitive balance? How do transfer systems, revenue sharing arrangements and salary caps affect competitive balance, player salaries, ticket prices and owners' profits?

1.3   OBJECTIVES OF CLUB OWNERS

In professional team sports, clubs can have different objectives and they lead to different outcomes in terms of distribution of talent among clubs in a league, player salary level, total league revenue, ticket price and so on. Also, the impact of most market regulations on these variables is different. The most common firm objective in economic theory is profit maximisation. In the United States, most analysts assume that professional sports clubs also behave as profit maximisers (Rottenberg, 1956; Noll, 1974c; Quirk and Fort, 1992; Vrooman, 1995). One of the most important decisions club managers have to make is the hiring of talent. More talents not only increase the season cost of a club but also the winning record and the season revenue. So clubs will hire the number of playing talents that maximises the difference between season revenue and season cost. If π indicates season profits, the objective is:

$$\max \pi = \max(R - C) \tag{1.1}$$

where R is total season revenue and C is total season cost. Assuming that the number of talents of the team is the only decision variable, the optimality condition for profit maximisation is that the marginal revenue of talent equals the marginal cost. A club maximises its profits if the increase in total revenue by hiring one more talent is equal to the increase in the total cost of one more talent. As long as the marginal revenue is higher than the marginal cost, the club can increase its profit by hiring more talent.

In Europe, sports economists have raised serious doubts about profit maximisation as a realistic objective in professional sports. Although professional sports clubs in the North American major leagues are more businesslike than in the European football leagues, some US economists seem to have their doubts as well (see Quirk and El-Hodiri, 1974; Rascher,

1997; Zimbalist, 2003). Sloane (1971) asserted that European football clubs do not behave as profit maximisers, but rather as utility maximisers. He observed that many owners of European football clubs consider spending money on their team as a consumption activity. As consumers, club owners act as if they are maximising a utility function where other variables, beside profits, appear as arguments; this might include playing success, stadium attendance, competitive balance, community building and so on.

One can also ask what the most important variable in Sloane's utility function is, as this is the crucial variable to be maximised. Késenne (1996, 2000a), in an attempt to make the utility-maximising model more operational, introduced win maximisation as the sole objective. Sports clubs are most of all interested in winning, and the best way to achieve that goal is to hire the best players, or in other words, to maximise the number of playing talents under certain restrictions. One restriction is that a club has to stay within the limits of its budget. As a first approximation, the breakeven condition can be imposed, that is, total revenue equals total cost. However, this condition is not necessary for the application of the win-maximisation model. It could be assumed that a club has to guarantee a certain profit rate in order to satisfy the owners or the shareholders, but a club can be profitable without being a profit maximiser. Also, the win-maximisation model does not exclude season losses because, as a consumer, the owner can be prepared to spend money on the team. In its most simple form, this objective function can be written as:

$$\max w \quad \text{subject to:} \quad R - C = \pi^0 \tag{1.2}$$

where w is the season winning percentage of the team and π^0 is a fixed amount of positive or negative profits. A fixed amount of profits also implies a fixed profit rate, because the capital stock is considered to be constant in the short run. So, the breakeven condition is only a special case where profits are zero. Win maximisation under the breakeven condition is also equivalent to constrained revenue maximisation as long as total club revenue is not reduced at a very high winning percentage.

Another variant of the utility maximisation model has been proposed by Rascher (1997), who assumed that sports clubs are maximising a linear combination of profits and wins, which can be written as:

$$\max (\pi + \alpha w) \quad \text{with } \alpha > 0. \tag{1.3}$$

Because the weight parameter α can be different for every club, it allows clubs to be more profit orientated or more win orientated. This model is comparable with the win-maximisation model, which also includes the possibility of a certain profit rate.

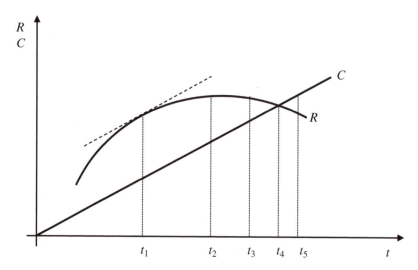

Figure 1.1   Club objectives

So far, all empirical tests have failed to be conclusive in accepting or rejecting the profit- or the win-maximisation hypothesis. To the best of our knowledge, all tests are based on the pricing rule or price elasticity (see Noll, 1974b; Ferguson *et al.*, 1991; Alexander, 2001), but as will be shown in Chapter 4, the pricing rule of a win-maximising club is the same as the pricing rule of a profit-maximising club.

Are these three objectives all that different? Is hiring the best players not the only way to increase the winning percentage, as well as club revenue and profits? A simple diagram shows that win and profit maximisation do make a difference in hiring the optimal number of playing talents. Figure 1.1 shows the different talent demand levels emerging from different club objectives. The number of talents is indicated on the horizontal axis and total season revenue and cost on the vertical axis. Obviously, the total cost increases with the number of talents. Also a club's total revenue increases as the club becomes more successful, but the revenue function is assumed to be concave in the number of talents. It decreases if the club becomes too strong and public interest fades because of a lack of uncertainty of outcome.

A profit-maximising club will hire t_1 playing talents, where marginal revenue, which is the slope of the revenue function, equals marginal cost, which is the slope of the cost function. A revenue maximiser will hire t_2 talents. A win-maximising club under the breakeven constraint will hire t_4 talents, where total cost equals total revenue. If a certain profit rate is necessary, the club can hire t_3 talents. If the owner is prepared to lose money on its team, he can hire t_5 talents.

EXERCISES 1

Assume the following quadratic revenue function and the linear cost function in terms of talents $R=10t-t^2$ and $C=2t$.

   Derive the optimal number of talents and also the profits of:

1.1. a profit maximiser

1.2. a revenue maximiser

1.3. a win maximiser

1.4. a maximiser of a linear combination of profits and wins with $a=3$.

2. Sports product market

2.1 INTRODUCTION

The product market in the professional team sports industry is the market of games and league championships. In most countries and professional sports disciplines, a monopoly league seems to be the rule. Whenever rival leagues show up in a country, they tend to merge after some time, or to cooperate and act as if they are one single league. Most sports economists, even advocates of more competition in sports, seem to accept this fact, and do not consider a monopoly league as necessarily anticompetitive (see Noll, 1999). In North American professional sports, all closed major leagues are monopoly leagues. In Europe, where multiple national leagues coexist, all structured hierarchically by a system of relegation to and promotion from lower divisions, the highest division in each country can be considered as a monopoly league. Notwithstanding the European Union and its common market for goods, services and capital, the national product markets of professional team sports are still protected from foreign competition. We will therefore only concentrate on the product market of games in a championship that is organised by a monopoly league. The producers and suppliers of the sports product are the clubs; the consumers and demanders of the sports product are the fans. The product can be purchased or consumed by attending a game in a stadium or by watching it on television. The stadium visitors pay a ticket price to enter the park. Watching a game on television can be free or paid for. Open-air television by state-owned companies is mainly paid by general taxation or a specific television tax. Privately owned broadcasting companies can attract television advertising, paid by different companies and industries to market their products, but can also charge a price; this can be the viewer's subscription fees or pay-per-view. Television companies can broadcast a full match, live or recorded, or only the highlights. In the following sections, we will first analyse the market of live sport followed by the market of televised sport.

2.2 MARKET OF LIVE SPORT

In almost every country, the product market of professional team sports is strictly regulated by the league, so it can be considered as a cartel of clubs (see Sloane, 1971). This is often justified by the peculiar economics of the industry. Although most economists accept that a certain degree of cooperation between the clubs in a league is inevitable, they do not agree with all regulations and restrictions that are imposed by the league, as will be explained later on.

One of the important restrictions is the lack of free entry to the market whatever the profitability of the participating clubs. The number of clubs in the North American major leagues or in the highest national divisions in the European countries is officially fixed, and can only be changed by a formal agreement between the clubs in the league. An interesting issue is the optimal number of clubs in a league, and the question is whether this number can be left to the participating clubs to decide. It is obvious that in most cases the insiders want to keep the outsider at bay, and that the stronger teams want to eliminate some of the weaker teams, certainly if revenues are shared among teams in a league. From the perspective of teams, leagues and society, it is not clear what the welfare implications of league contraction are (see Noll, 2003).

Another restriction is that clubs are not free to choose their locations. In most US major leagues and European national leagues, clubs are not free to move without formal permission from the league. This has serious consequences because it gives the clubs in large cities a permanent advantage over those in small towns. It also forces an ambitious club to stay in its small market. An important consequence of this restriction is not only that it can cause a lasting competitive imbalance in a league, but also that most clubs are local monopolists in their region.

Some of these regulations can be countered, to a certain extent, by the European system of relegation and promotion, whereby the teams at the bottom of the final ranking in each division are relegated to a lower division, and the champions of the lower divisions are promoted to a higher division. This way, the local monopoly position of a team in a large market, or a region with a large drawing potential, can be broken. Relegation and promotion also create more incentives for the low-ranked teams to perform because demotion to a lower division often implies a dramatic budget reduction (see Noll, 2002).

Clubs are also not free to determine their production output and the supply of their product on the market. It is the league that organises the championship and decides when, where and how many times teams have to play. These restrictions do not seem to bother most economists because they agree that a well-organised championship is far more interesting for fans to watch than a number of random matches.

In this section, we will describe and analyse a club's revenue and cost functions, concentrating on stadium attendance and gate receipts. The model will then be used to analyse ticket pricing. Before we describe the demand for tickets, we will first address one of the central issues in sports economics, which is competitive balance and the uncertainty of outcome.

2.2.1   Uncertainty of Outcome and Competitive Balance

The importance of uncertainty of outcome or competitive balance in a league, is one of the most discussed and controversial issues in sports economics. Competition on the playing field is a basic ingredient of sports. In the literature, three levels of uncertainty of outcome have been distinguished: match uncertainty, seasonal uncertainty or within-season uncertainty, and championship uncertainty or between-season uncertainty (see Cairns, Jennett and Sloane, 1986; Kringstad and Gerrard, 2007; Sanderson, 2002; Szymanski, 2003).

Match uncertainty is often measured by looking at the square of the difference in winning percentages or league standings of the two clubs. The idea is that if the winning percentages of the two teams are too far apart, there is less uncertainty of outcome, which reduces fan interest. Jennett (1984) developed a within-season measure of uncertainty, which he used to explain match attendance. It indicates not only whether both teams are still in the running to win the championship, but also takes into account the number of games left before the closing of the championship.

Seasonal uncertainty is often approached by a parameter that is linked to the standard deviation (SD) of the winning percentages of the teams in the league. The smaller the SD, the smaller is the spread of winning percentages and the closer the competition. Because the SD, with an equal degree of imbalance, increases with the number of games played, the Noll–Scully SD ratio, which corrects for the number of games, is often used. It is given by $SD/0.5/\sqrt{m}$ where m is the number of games played. The denominator measures the 'ideal' (perfect balance) SD. This 'ideal' SD is based on a binomial distribution of the number of games won (see Fort and Quirk, 1995). A problem with the Noll–Scully SD ratio is not only that it cannot be applied if the games allow ties, but also that it can be, in some applications, significantly smaller then one, whereas theoretically, its minimum value is one. Indeed, a perfect balance means that all teams have the same winning percentage, so the 'ideal' SD is zero. A more appropriate and elegant measure has been proposed by Goossens (2006), which is the ratio of the actual SD and the SD in the case of a perfect imbalance or a perfect predictability of outcome. The value of this indicator, which she named NAMSI (National Measure of Seasonal Imbalance), lies between zero and one. The closer to zero, the higher is the seasonal uncertainty. The advantages of this measure are that comparisons can be made between leagues with a different number of teams and games, and that it is also applicable in championships allowing ties.

Championship uncertainty is a dynamic measure, and adds another element to the notion of uncertainty of outcome by taking into account more than one season. Even if, over a number of consecutive seasons, the standard deviations of the winning percentages are always the same, it can hide totally different situations. One possibility is that the same teams always end up on top; another is that in each season another team ends up on top. A simple way to measure this uncertainty is to count the number of different teams that reach the top or the top three positions in the final ranking over a number of seasons. Humphreys (2002) has tried to combine seasonal uncertainty and championship uncertainty in one single measure, called the competitive balance ratio. A disadvantage of this ratio is that important information on the kind of imbalance is lost.

Extensive empirical research on the demand for tickets has shown that the estimation results of the impact on attendance of match uncertainty and seasonal uncertainty are not very significant and robust. So far, although few empirical tests exist, championship uncertainty turns out to have a more significant positive effect on attendance. Apparently, fans don't like to see the same clubs on top year after year (see Borland and Macdonald, 2003; Forrest and Simmons, 2002; Garcia and Rodriguez, 2002; Krautmann and Hadley, 2004).

2.2.2 Stadium Attendance

In explaining stadium attendance, one can distinguish between at least two different approaches. Besides the study of the season attendance of a club, one can also be interested in explaining the number of tickets sold for each single game. Depending on that choice, other explanatory variables have to be taken into account.

Season attendance

The total season attendance of a club depends first of all on the characteristics of its local market. It is obvious that the drawing potential for spectators of a team in a large city, or a densely populated area, is greater than in a small town. However, it is not only the size of the population that is important; preferences and social stratification can also affect the purchase of stadium tickets. We bring these characteristics together in one variable which we call the size of the market or the drawing potential of the team. We assume that this variable cannot be controlled by club management, so all considerations regarding a club's marketing policy are left out.

A second variable that is considered very important for club attendance is the performance of the team on the field or its playing success. This variable can be measured by the season winning percentage of the team or its ranking. Fans clearly prefer winning teams over losing teams. However, the winning percentage of a team should not become too high. If a team becomes too strong compared with its opponents so that the probability of winning approaches unity, there is no longer any uncertainty of outcome in the league championship. Because this can have a negative effect on public interest, the attendance function is assumed to be concave in a team's winning percentage. Winning has a diminishing marginal effect on the demand for tickets. If the winning percentage passes a certain critical value, its effect on attendances can even be negative, so one can assume that the revenue function is not only concave but also first increasing and then decreasing in relation to the winning percentage.

As explained in the previous section, uncertainty of outcome (*uo*) can also be introduced into the demand function model by a more specific variable. One simple indicator is $uo = w(1 - w)$, where *w* is the season winning percentage of a team. This variable reaches it maximum value (*uo* = 0.25) with maximum uncertainty (*w* = 0.5). It follows that both variables, the winning percentage and the uncertainty of outcome can be represented in the attendance function by *w*. Moreover, if the supporters' trade-off between winning percentage and uncertainty of outcome is given by the product of the two variables, or utility $u = w^2 (1 - w)$, one can derive that the optimal winning percentage is larger than 0.5, because $\partial u/\partial w = 2w - 3w^2 = 0$, so $w^0 = 0.67$ (see also Sandy, Sloane and Rosentraub, 2004).

Besides the relative quality of a team, measured by the winning percentage, its absolute playing quality can also affect a club's season attendance. It makes a difference to fans if their home team is the best in a high-quality league or the best in a low-quality league. Spectators like to watch the spectacular performances of the star players even if these stars play for the visiting team. So, the absolute playing quality in the league can be measured by the total sum of talents in the league. In a short-term model, however, this variable can be assumed to be constant, and the same for every team, so it is left out of the model in this section.

The ticket price is also likely to affect the demand for tickets. If sport is a normal good, the lower the ticket price, *ceteris paribus*, the more tickets will be sold. Obviously, most clubs charge different ticket prices, depending on the position and the comfort of the stadium seat. Clubs also sell season tickets, which reduce the price for attending one game. For simplicity reasons, we only take one ticket price into consideration, which can be considered as the average price to enter the ballpark.

So, the attendance function can be specified as:

$$A_i = A_i[m_i, w_i, p_i] \qquad \text{for all } i: 1, n, \tag{2.1}$$

where A_i is the season stadium attendance of club i, m_i is the size of its local market, w_i is the season winning percentage of the team, p_i is the average ticket price and n is the number of teams. Based on the discussion above, the following conditions hold for this demand functions:

$$\frac{\partial A_i}{\partial m_i} > 0 \qquad \frac{\partial A_i}{\partial p_i} < 0$$

$$\frac{\partial A_i}{\partial w_i} > 0 \quad \text{for } w_i < w^0 \quad \text{and} \quad \frac{\partial A_i}{\partial w_i} < 0 \quad \text{for } w_i > w_i^0 \tag{2.2}$$

$$\frac{\partial^2 A_i}{\partial w_i^2} < 0,$$

where w^0 is an exogenously given critically high winning percentage.

Match attendance

One can also be interested in the variables that explain the attendance of an individual game. In this approach, beside the size of the market and the winning percentage of the home team, other factors have to be taken into consideration. First of all, a distinction has to be made between the home and away games. It makes a difference if team x is playing against team y in the large home market of team x or in the small home market of team y. An additional explanatory variable might be the winning percentage of the visiting team. On the one hand, referring to the uncertainty of outcome, the closeness between the two teams can have a positive effect on match attendance, so the squared difference between the winning percentages matters. However, as mentioned above, this effect does not get much empirical support. On the other hand, fans love to watch their team playing against a top team, not only because it promises to be a high-quality game, but also because it is a thrill to see a moderate team beating a top team. The winning percentage of the visiting team can also be seen as an indicator of the absolute quality of the match. One might also consider including the size of the market of the visiting team and the distance between the markets of the two teams. For instance, if the distance between the teams is not large, as in some small European countries, the visiting team can bring its own supporters. In the North American major leagues, however, its effect is less important. So the demand function for tickets of a single game can be specified as:

$$A_{ij} = A_{ij}[m_i, w_i, w_j, p_i] \quad \text{for all } i, j \quad i \neq j, \tag{2.3}$$

where A_{ij} is the number of spectators attending the game of home team i playing against visiting team j. The signs of the market size and the home winning percentage are the same as in (2.2); the winning percentage of the visiting team can be expected to have a positive effect on match attendance.

The relationship between season attendance and game attendance of all teams is then simply:

$$A_i = \sum_{j \neq i}^{n} A_{ij} \quad \text{for all } i.$$

The estimation of this (indirect) specification of the season attendance function can yield more information than the (direct) specification of the season demand function in (2.1), but it also needs a considerably larger data set.

2.2.3   Club Revenue and Cost

Stadium attendances determine a club's gate receipts, which are simply the number of tickets sold multiplied by the average ticket price. The total season revenue of a modern sports club, however, does not only depend on ticket sales. Over the last decades, the share of gate receipts in the budget of a club has diminished. Broadcasting rights and commercial income, such as sponsorship, merchandising and licensing, have gradually taken over. Nevertheless, there seems to be a positive correlation between the sum of commercial and broadcasting revenues, on the one hand, and stadium attendances, on the other. Sponsors, as well as the merchandising business, are more interested in successful clubs with many spectators. Also, television companies prefer to broadcast games that are watched by many people. If this positive correlation seems to be obvious for commercial revenue, it is less so for broadcast revenue. However, even if a broadcast game has a negative effect on stadium attendance, its greater exposure increases the clubs' commercial income. Moreover, empirical studies show that it is not very clear whether televised and live games are substitutes or complements (see Siegfried and Hinshaw, 1979; Simmons and Buraimo, 2005). So, in order to simplify the analysis, we assume in this model that the sum of all non-gate receipts of a club is proportional to the club's stadium attendance. The value of the proportionality factor can differ between clubs. It will also be different in each national league, depending on the size of the national market and the international reputation of the league. Gate receipts are dominantly determined by the size of the local market; however, television rights, sponsoring and merchandising are determined by the size of the national market. If κ_i is the proportionality factor, total season revenue of a club is then equal to the sum of gate receipts $P_i A_i$ and all other revenues $\kappa_i A_i$ and can be specified as:

$$R_i = (p_i + \kappa_i) A_i[m_i, w_i, p_i] = R_i[m_i, w_i, p_i] \qquad \kappa_i > 0 \tag{2.4}$$

Based on the conditions of the attendance function as given in (2.2), the following conditions hold for the revenue function:

$$\frac{\partial R_i}{\partial m_i} = (p + \kappa_i)\frac{\partial A_i}{\partial m_i} > 0$$

$$\frac{\partial R_i}{\partial w_i} = (p_i + \kappa_i)\frac{\partial A_i}{\partial w_i} > \text{or} < 0 \qquad \text{if} \qquad \frac{\partial A_i}{\partial w_i} > \text{or} < 0 \qquad (2.5)$$

$$\frac{\partial^2 R_i}{\partial w_i^2} = (p_i + \kappa_i)\frac{\partial^2 A_i}{\partial w_i^2} < 0.$$

The impact of a change in the ticket price on total season revenue is more complicated. A higher ticket price lowers attendance, but it increases the revenue per attendee. If revenue only consists of ticket sales, a well-known result from microeconomic theory is that the effect of the price change on revenue depends on the value of price elasticity of the demand for tickets. The price elasticity $\varepsilon_i = -(\partial A_i/\partial p_i)(p_i/A_i)$ is the ratio of the percentage change in attendance and the percentage change in the price. If the price elasticity is larger than one, the price has a negative effect on revenue; if the price elasticity is smaller than one, the price has a positive effect on revenue; if the price elasticity is equal to one, a price change has no effect on revenue.

If there are more revenue sources then just ticket sales, as in revenue function (2.4), the price effect can be calculated as:

$$\frac{\partial R_i}{\partial p_i} = A_i + (p_i + \kappa_i)\frac{\partial A_i}{\partial p_i} = A_i\left(1 - \varepsilon_i / \frac{p_i}{p_i + \kappa_i}\right).$$

From this expression it can be derived that the effect of the ticket price on total revenue is positive (negative) if the price elasticity is smaller (larger) than $p_i/(p_i + \kappa_i)$. This last ratio is clearly smaller than one, and decreases with the importance of the non-gate receipts. If the non-gate receipts become the dominant revenue source, the ticket price will only have a positive effect on club revenue if the price elasticity of ticket demand is very low. This can be explained by the fact that a price increase will not only lower attendances, but also a club's commercial and broadcasting revenue.

On the cost side of many clubs, the players or the playing talents are the most important factors of production, and the largest share of total season expenditures is spent on player salaries. There is obviously a close relationship between the talents of the team and its winning percentage, but this will be discussed in Chapter 3.

The player labour cost can be calculated as the number of a team's playing talents (not the number of players, as will be explained in Chapter 3) multiplied by the unit cost of talent. Besides the player salaries, club owners who also own their stadium face a considerable capital cost, which is a fixed cost in the short run. If all other cost elements are neglected in this model, the total season cost function of a club can simply be written as:

$$C_i = c_i t_i + c_i^0 \tag{2.6}$$

where c_i^0 is the fixed capital cost and c_i the marginal unit cost of talent. If the player labour market is competitive, the market clearing cost of a unit of talent will be the same for every club, so that in (2.6) $c_i = c$ for all i. Vrooman (1995) introduced a more general cost function where the marginal cost of talent can be different for each team and where the market size can also affect the cost of talent. In the following chapters, however, we will use the simplified specification above. This specification of the cost function also implies that the marginal cost of spectators is zero, that is, $\partial C_i / \partial A_i = 0$, which seems to be a plausible assumption. One more spectator in the stadium does not increase the total cost of the club in any significant way, so the marginal cost is extremely small and will be set to zero in this model.

2.2.4   Ticket Pricing

In most industries, where many producers are competing to sell their products to many consumers, the price of the products is determined by the market. The law of demand and supply fixes the market-clearing equilibrium price level. The question is whether this is also true in the professional team sports industry. One of the important consequences of leagues' regulations on the product market is that most clubs are local monopolists. Some exceptions exist in very large US cities or densely populated areas, or in Europe, where the relegation and promotion system can bring two clubs of the same city into the highest division. Fan loyalty in sports, however, makes the application of a duopoly model rather questionable.

From economic theory, we know that profit-maximising monopoly holders tend to increase prices above and reduce output below Pareto-optimum values. Whereas in a competitive product market firms are price takers, the single firm in a monopoly market is a price maker. As a local monopolist, a sports club faces the downward-sloping market demand curve for its tickets, so it can set the ticket price at a level which realises its objective of profit or win maximisation.

To show the implications step by step, we will first consider a model where a club's only revenue is the sale of tickets, so that κ_i in revenue function (2.4) equals zero, and where the ticket price is the only decision variable, given a fixed number of talents. What will the optimal ticket price be if the club is a **profit maximiser**? Dropping the subscripts, the club's profit function can now be written as:

$$\pi = pA - C.$$

In order to find the optimal ticket price, the partial derivative of the profit function with respect to the ticket price has to equal zero:

$$\frac{\partial \pi}{\partial p} = p \frac{\partial A}{\partial p} + A = 0 \tag{2.7}$$

Because the marginal cost of spectators is assumed to be zero, a change in the ticket price does not affect the club's total cost. Applying the chain rule, and given that the marginal cost of spectators is zero:

$$\frac{\partial C}{\partial p} = \frac{\partial C}{\partial A} \frac{\partial A}{\partial p} = 0.$$

It follows that the profit maximisation condition is equivalent to the revenue maximisation condition. The optimal ticket price is found where:

$$\varepsilon = -\frac{\partial A}{\partial p} \frac{p}{A} = 1,$$

so profits are maximised at the point where the price elasticity equals one.

Assuming that the demand function $A[m, p, w]$ can be drawn as a linear function of the ticket price, Figure 2.1 presents a downward-sloping demand curve. As can easily be derived, the price elasticity equals one in point E, exactly at the middle of the linear demand curve because $A/p = -\partial A/\partial p$. The optimal price is p_1 and A_1 spectators buy a ticket. At the upper (lower) part of the demand function, the price elasticity is larger (smaller) than one.

In fixing the optimal ticket price, it is possible that the club manager faces a stadium capacity constraint. The optimal ticket price under this condition can now be found at the point of intersection of the demand curve and the capacity constraint. If the stadium cannot receive more than A^0 spectators, as indicated in Figure 2.1, a profit maximising owner will set the ticket price at p_2 above p_1.

We now extend the pricing model by including also the non-gate revenue and investigate if this changes the optimal ticket price. A profit-maximising club will set the ticket price that maximises total revenue:

$$\frac{\partial \pi}{\partial p} = (p + \kappa) \frac{\partial A}{\partial p} + A = 0 \qquad \text{or} \qquad \varepsilon = \frac{p}{p + \kappa} < 1. \tag{2.8}$$

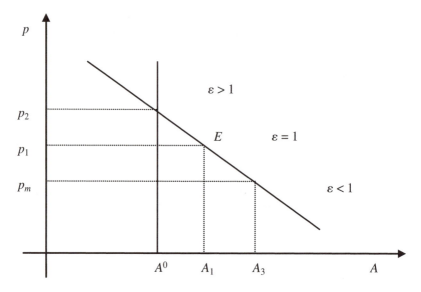

Figure 2.1   Demand for tickets

It follows that the optimal ticket price is now set where the price elasticity is smaller than one, so that, given the same demand curve for tickets as depicted in Figure 2.1, the optimal ticket price is found in the inelastic part of the demand curve. A lower ticket price will be set than in the model with only gate receipts. With a lower ticket price, stadium attendance will be higher, as will be all non-gate revenues that are proportional to attendance. It follows that profits will also be higher.

If most clubs in professional sports leagues are local monopolists in the product market, they are price makers and can set ticket prices above the social optimum level. League authorities, however, can impose maximum ticket prices. How does this affect club behaviour? In Figure 2.1, the profit-maximising ticket price is given by p_1. If the league imposes a maximum ticket price of p_m, it is obvious that this will have a positive effect on attendance. The imposed maximum price will increase attendance from A_1 to A_3, which will also lower a club's season revenue and profit.

An interesting question is how an increase in the cost of playing talent affects the optimal ticket price. Club owners often argue that player salaries should be under control in order to keep ticket prices low so that people with moderate income can also afford to attend the games. This sounds reasonable. However, if clubs are local monopolists in the product market and the marginal cost of spectators is zero, lower salaries will not lower the optimal ticket prices. Solving the equations (2.7) or (2.8) for the optimal ticket price, it is clear that the cost of talent does not appear in this solution. So, a profit-maximising club will not change its ticket price if player salaries are lowered. Decreasing the unit cost of playing talent, with a constant number of playing talents, will only lower a club's total cost and increase its profits (see Noll, 1974c).

What if clubs are **win maximisers**? Referring to objective (1.2), the only way a club manager can maximise the winning percentage of his team is by hiring as many talents as can be afforded within the limits of the budget. However, in this first version of the model, we have assumed that the number of talents is fixed and that the ticket price is the only decision variable. It follows that the win-maximisation model does not apply here. The ticket price decision of a win-maximising club will be addressed using a two-decision variable model in Chapter 4.

2.3 MARKET OF TELEVISION RIGHTS AND TELEVISION SPORT

It is not necessary to go to the ball park to watch a game. Sports have become a very popular media product, in particular on television. In many countries all over the world, sports get the highest spectator ratings. On the one hand, many sports became popular as a spectator sport because they were broadcast worldwide, and broadcasting rights have become one of the major sources of club revenue. On the other hand, television advertising before, during and after broadcast sports events has become one of the most important revenue sources of television companies. Television is one of the most important channels for international companies to market their products. However, this relationship between sports and the media has also raised many questions and problems (see Jeanrenaud and Késenne, 2006).

2.3.1 Demand for Television Sport

One of the questions concerns the demand for television sport. In the case of free-to-air television, the additional price, or the marginal cost of watching a game on television is very low. In the case of a pay channel, or pay-per-view, the price can be high. This raises the question of the extent to which live sport and television sport are substitutes or complements. The answer can only be given by empirical research. Apart from the complications raised by delayed television coverage or by broadcasting only the highlights of a game, the theoretical set-up of this research, as well as the specification of the demand function, is crucial for the interpretation of the results. It is obvious, for instance, that the number of spectators of a particular game can hardly be higher if that game is broadcast live. So, a dummy variable as an additional explanatory variable in attendance function (2.1), with the value of one if the game is broadcast, will probably yield a negative coefficient. Does it mean that stadium sport and television sport are substitutes? If season attendance is investigated, it is perfectly possible that a sport becomes more popular because it is broadcast, so more spectators are also interested in experiencing it live. A good illustration of this phenomenon is that some less popular sport disciplines have to pay, and are willing to pay, to be televised instead of being paid. The more conventional way to test whether products are substitutes or complements is to estimate the cross-price elasticity. If the price of watching sports on television (p_s) is added as an explanatory variable in demand curve (2.1), the answer depends on the sign of the price effect:

$$\frac{\partial A[m, w, p, p_s]}{\partial p_s}.$$

If this price effect is positive, televised sport and live sport are substitutes; if it is negative, they are complements.

Even if broadcasting more games reduces stadium attendance, it is still possible that more broadcasting increases club revenue because the loss of stadium attendance can be more than compensated for by the increase of television rights. If the marginal cost of watching a game on television is very low, it will also attract a different public from the regular and loyal supporters who come to the stadium.

Another major concern is that the fast-growing market of televised sports, and the money that goes with it, threaten the necessary competitive balance in professional team sports. This has always been one of the main arguments for sports federations to monopolise the sale of broadcasting rights to television companies. A free and competitive market of broadcasting rights, where the individual clubs could sell the rights to their home games, would concentrate all the TV money in the most successful clubs, because spectators are only interested in watching the best teams. The pooling of TV rights by the sports federation, so the argument goes, is necessary to have the television money distributed among all clubs in the league according to a chosen redistribution key. Economists, however, do not like monopolies because they cause prices to be too high and output to be too low compared with competitive markets. This can be seen in Figure 2.2, where the competitive market equilibrium is compared with the monopolist's equilibrium. The profit-maximising point of the monopolist is given by E_1 at the point of intersection of the marginal revenue and the marginal cost curves. The competitive market

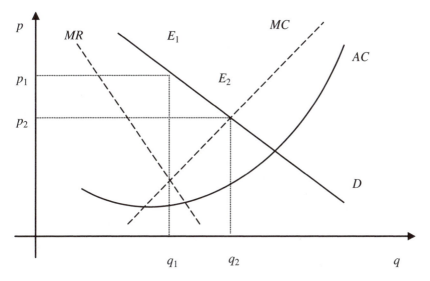

Figure 2.2   Monopoly versus perfect competition

equilibrium is given by E_2, where the market demand and supply curves ($= MC$) intersect. The monopoly price is clearly higher and the monopoly output is lower.

Considering the outcomes of competition and monopoly, the question can be raised whether the arguments of the leagues are strong enough to justify the pooling of TV rights. First of all, the empirical evidence, showing that the public turns away from an unbalanced competition, is not very convincing, although it is still unclear what kind and what degree of imbalance one is dealing with, and how it should be measured (see Borland and Macdonald, 2003). Based on empirical research, Szymanski and Leach (2005) even assert that the competitive balance that emerges from a competitive player market, without any restrictions or revenue sharing arrangements, is more balanced than the public's revealed preference.

Moreover, in some countries several courts have called the pooling of TV rights illegal, and in contravention of the European competition laws. Not the federation but the clubs are the legal owners of the TV rights of their home games. Although the issue is far from settled legally, one can argue from an economic point of view that it should be a shared ownership. The reason is that the value of a match that is part of a well-organised league championship is much higher than the value of an occasional friendly game between two clubs. It follows that part of the TV money belongs to the organising league, and should be redistributed among the teams. This argument goes back to one of the peculiarities of the professional team sports industry (see Chapter 1).

A consequence of pooling is also that, once the rights are granted to just one broadcasting company, a new monopoly position is created in the market of televised sport. So, a distinction should be made between the market of TV rights, on the one hand, where the sports clubs or the federation are on the supply side and the television companies on the demand side, and the market of televised sports, on the other hand, where the television companies are on the supply side and the TV spectators on the demand side. So, if pay-per-view is an option, the price can again be too high, and the output of broadcast games too low, compared with a market where many broadcasters hold the broadcasting rights of the matches.

Finally, some politicians argue that a national pastime, such as baseball in the US or football in Europe, showing some characteristics of a public good, should be broadcast over the air and not be hidden behind an expensive decoder.

In the following sections, we will analyse both the market of TV rights and the market of televised sport. First, we deal with the market of TV rights and investigate if, and under what conditions, the pooling argument of the sports federations holds, and if the objective of balanced competition can be guaranteed without monopolising the market. Then we deal with the market of televised sport. Will a profit-maximising television company that is granted the exclusive TV rights choose pay-per-view or free-to-air?

2.3.2   Pooling of Broadcasting Rights

In the literature, two arguments can be found in favour of a collective sale of television rights by the league authorities (see Noll, 1999). The first one is that some redistribution of club revenue is necessary in order to guarantee a reasonable competitive balance in the league championship, because broadcasting rights have become an increasing and already dominant revenue source in many countries. However, the question can be raised whether monopolising the rights is necessary to redistribute the TV money. The answer is clearly negative. The league could allow the individual sale of all games by each home team and take action afterwards to collect a certain percentage of the clubs' revenue and redistribute the money. The next question then is which regime, collective or individual selling, will generate the highest broadcasting net revenue that can be distributed or redistributed. This brings us to the second argument in favour of pooling. The individual sale of the rights by all clubs would imply high transaction costs because of intensive bargaining between all clubs and all broadcasters for all matches. Higher transaction costs reduce the net revenue of decentralised selling. To a certain extent, however, this unfavourable effect can be countered by the positive incentives that are created by the fierce competition between clubs, so that more effort is made to get more TV money. The comfortable monopoly position of the league can also induce a rather ease-loving attitude and might create an ineffective bureaucracy and less cost-effective procedures.

If one starts from a market of matches that qualify to be televised, with clubs and league on the supply side and television companies on the demand side, it is hard to see how decentralized selling can beat pooled selling in the collection of broadcast revenue. The main reason is that the total cost of selling the TV rights by a monopoly league is not only low but also fixed, that is, they are independent of the quantity of TV rights that are sold. If all costs consist mainly of fixed costs, the marginal cost is (close to) zero. The total cost is also low because the selling of the TV rights includes only the cost of bargaining with the television companies about who gets the exclusive broadcast rights to all the games. Broadcast or not, the matches are played anyway. It follows that, with a given downward-sloping demand curve for TV rights and zero marginal cost, a profit-maximising sports league will set the price and sell the number of broadcasting rights that maximise league revenue. Given the low cost of bargaining, the league's net revenue can hardly be lower than the net revenue from the decentralised selling of TV rights in a competitive market. In the case of decentralised selling, with the same market demand curve for TV rights, any other point on the demand curve than the one chosen by the league will yield a lower level of total league revenue. Also, with the higher transaction costs of decentralised selling by all individual clubs dealing with many television companies discussing the price of every individual game, net revenue can be expected to be lower.

If the pooling of broadcasting rights is favourable for league and club revenue, it is not necessarily favourable for the supporters. A possible consequence of pooling, compared with decentralised selling, is that the price the television companies have to pay per match is higher and that the number of televised matches is lower. Does this negative effect of a monopoly market necessarily occur in the market of TV rights?

Assume that the broadcasters' demand for TV rights q_r is a linear function of the price of the rights p_r:

$$p_r = \alpha - \beta q_r.$$

If the marginal cost of centralised sale of the TV rights by the league is zero, the profit-maximising equilibrium is found where total revenue is maximised, that is, where marginal revenue equals zero, so that:

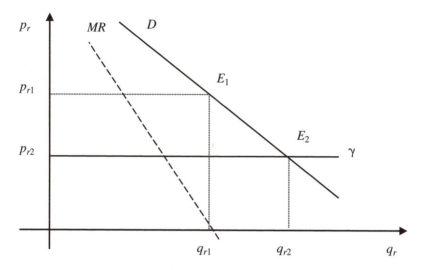

Figure 2.3   Pooling of TV rights versus decentralised selling

$$q_{r1} = \frac{\alpha}{2\beta} \quad \text{and} \quad p_{r1} = \frac{\alpha}{2}.$$

In the case of decentralized selling by the individual clubs, the marginal transaction cost is clearly different from zero, say $\gamma > 0$, so the equilibrium price and output in the competitive market can be found as the solution of: $\alpha - \beta q_r = \gamma$, so:

$$q_{r2} = \frac{\alpha - \gamma}{\beta} \quad \text{and} \quad p_{r2} = \gamma.$$

From this we can conclude that pooling will only result in a higher output and a lower price in the unlikely case of $\alpha < 2\gamma$. Indeed, α is a price that is so high that no TV company would be interested in buying the rights to one single game.

Figure 2.3 illustrates this case. If the downward-sloping demand curve for TV rights is given by D and the marginal transaction cost in the case of decentralised selling by the horizontal line γ, the equilibrium is reached at point E_2. If the league is monopolising the TV rights and sells the rights in a package deal to just one broadcaster, the optimum is found in point E_1, where $MR = MC = 0$. In this case, with $\alpha > 2\gamma$, one can see that the price of the TV rights is higher and the number of broadcast games lower if the TV rights are pooled by the league.

However, games are not homogenous products; they are all of different quality. But if only the games between top teams are taken into account, and these games can all be expected to be of high quality, this model can serve as a first approximation for analysing the market of broadcast rights.

The conclusion from this section is that the pooling of broadcasting rights will probably enhance the total broadcasting revenue of the league, so that there is more money to share among the clubs, but it might also result in higher prices and lower output due to monopolistic price setting. So, in a welfare-economic approach, what is good for the clubs and what is good for the supporters should be weighed against each other. If there are good arguments for sharing the broadcasting rights, the pooling of the rights is not a necessary condition for sharing.

2.3.3 Pay-Per-View or Free-to-Air?

As mentioned in the previous section, one of the disadvantages of pooling television rights is that, in many cases, they are sold in a package deal to just one broadcaster, which becomes a monopolist in the market of televised games, not only for selling the matches by pay-per-view, but also for selling TV slots to advertisers. Again, higher prices and lower output will reduce the spectators' real income and welfare.

If a private and profit-maximising broadcaster has managed to get the exclusive rights to broadcast all games, will it choose pay-per-view or free-to-air? A TV company has at least two revenue sources. As a monopolist, it is facing a downward-sloping market demand curve for pay-per-view sport, but the television company is also collecting money from advertising. Before, during and after the match, paid advertising slots can be inserted. The more spectators are expected to watch, the more advertisers are willing to pay, so advertising revenue can be considered to be a positive function of the number of spectators. On the cost side, there are, beside the cost of the broadcasting rights, the operational costs of equipment, transportation and personnel. Both these cost categories are independent of the number of spectators, so the marginal cost is zero. The more spectators, however, the lower will be the average cost.

Given this scenario, the profit-maximising broadcaster has to make a choice: if he chooses free-to-air television, more spectators will watch, so more advertising money can be collected. In the case of pay-per-view, fewer spectators are willing to pay, so advertising revenue will also be lower. Which policy will maximise his profits? A simplified model can help to find out (see Van der Burg, 1996).

Assume that the demand for paid television sport is given by the linear function $p_s = \alpha - \beta q_s$, where p_s is the price per view and q_s is the number of spectators, and that the total revenue from advertising is a linear function of the number of spectators with parameter γ, so total revenue can be written as:

$$R_s = (\alpha + \gamma)q_s - \beta q_s^2.$$

Given a constant total cost C_s^0, the marginal cost is zero and the average cost is C_s^0/q_s. As a monopolist, the profit maximising company can set the optimal price, so the number of spectators is $q_s = (\alpha+\gamma)/2\beta$ and $p_s = (\alpha-\gamma)/2$. The optimal price is positive if $\alpha > \gamma$. Total profits can then be calculated as:

$$\pi_{s1} = R_{s1} - C_s^0 = \frac{(\alpha + \gamma)^2}{4\beta} - C_s^0.$$

In the free-to-air scenario, the price per view is zero, so the number of spectators $q_s = \alpha/\beta$ and total profits are:

$$\pi_{s2} = R_{a2} - C_s^0 = \frac{\gamma\alpha}{\beta} - C_s^0.$$

One can see that profits under pay-per-view are higher than under free-to-air. Subtracting the profits one finds that:

$$\pi_{s1} - \pi_{s2} = \frac{(\alpha - \gamma)^2}{4\beta},$$

so whatever the value of the parameters, the difference is positive. It implies that whatever the price-effect on demand, and whatever the sensitivity of the advertisers for the number of spectators, pay-per-view yields the highest profit level. However, the difference between both profit levels will be smaller, the smaller the price effect and the larger the response of advertisers.

Figure 2.4 illustrates this result. If the market demand for televised sport is given by curve D and if, on top of the pay-per view revenue, the broadcaster also collects the average revenue γ from advertising, the average revenue function becomes AR. The marginal revenue curve is then MR. The average cost curve is AC. If the broadcasting company chooses pay-per-view, the equilibrium point is found where $MR = MC = 0$, so it charges a price of p_{s1} and q_{s1} spectators are willing to pay the price. The average cost is then ac_1, so total profit is q_{s1} times the average profit (difference between ar_1 and ac_1).

If the broadcaster chooses free-to-air, the equilibrium is found at the level of demand with zero price, so q_{s2} spectators are watching. In this case,

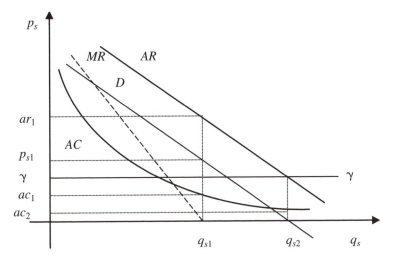

Figure 2.4　Pay-per-view versus free-to-air

the income from advertising is much higher but it is the only revenue source. Total profit is equal to q_{s2} times the average profit (difference between γ and the average cost ac_2). As shown above, total profit in this case will be lower.

The question can be raised why not every television company chooses pay-per-view or hides TV sports behind a decoder. One obvious answer is that most public television channels do not behave as profit maximisers; they often try to reach the highest possible number of spectators. However, many private companies also broadcast free-to-air sports. One explanation here is that some governments simply forbid pay-per-view, because of the generally accepted idea that a national pastime, as some sports are, should not be hidden behind a decoder. There might also be the threat of a public boycott of the pay channel. Another explanation is that the league may only grant the rights to a candidate under the condition of free-to-air broadcasting. There is at least one good reason for the league to do so: clubs and federations are also financially supported by other sponsors for shirt and board advertising. These advertisers can threaten to withdraw their support in the case of pay-per-view broadcasting, because it reduces the number of spectators and the impact of their marketing efforts.

The competition in the market of televised sport is linked to the competitive conditions in the market of TV rights. The pooling of TV rights often leads to exclusive broadcasting rights for one company, but not necessarily so. The league does not have to sell the whole package to one candidate but can sell the rights of the different teams or matches to different applicants. So, in the market of televised sports as well, the question must be asked whether granting the exclusive rights to all matches to one broadcaster is good for the supporters. Exclusivity again creates a monopoly with its negative consequences. If the market of televised sports is made more competitive, the pay-per-view price will approach the marginal cost, which is zero. In that case, marginal and average revenue are constant, because there is only advertising revenue, and average cost decreases with the number of spectators. So each television company can maximise its profits by maximising its number of spectators.

EXERCISES 2

2.1. Assume that gate receipts are a club's only source of revenue and that the demand function for tickets is given by $A = 5 - 0.5p$. The cost function is $C = 2t$. Attendances are measured in 10 000 fans and prices are in Euro.
- Calculate the optimal ticket price, the number of spectators and the total revenue of a profit-maximising club.
- Assuming that the stadium can only hold 20 000 spectators, what will the optimal ticket price and total revenue be?

2.2. For the same club as in exercise 2.1, and assuming other revenues besides gate receipts, but proportional to attendances with proportionality factor $\kappa = 4$, derive the optimal ticket price, the number of spectators and total club revenue with and without the stadium capacity constraint that the maximum number of spectators is 20 000.

2.3. For the same club as in exercise 2.1, and assuming that the league is imposing a maximum ticket price of 2 Euro, what will the number of spectators and the club's revenue be?

2.4. For a profit-maximising club with gate receipts as the only revenue source, the demand function for stadium tickets is given by $A = 5 - 0.5p$. Let the cost of talent be given by $C = ct$ with $t = 4$. Calculate the club's profit for different ticket prices, ranging from 3 to 7, and for different unit costs of talent, ranging from 2 to 4. What do you observe with respect to the relationship between the cost of talent and the optimal ticket price?

2.5. Assume that a TV company's demand curve for broadcasting rights is given by $p_r = 12 - 2q_r$. If the total cost is fixed at $C = 3$, calculate the optimal price, the quantity sold and the profit of a league that is pooling the TV rights and tries to maximise profits.

2.6. With the same demand function as in exercise 2.5, calculate the optimal price, quantity and revenue in a competitive market if the total cost function is given by $C = 2 + 0.2q_r^2$. Compare the results with the results of exercise 2.5. What do you conclude?

2.7. Assume that a broadcasting company's revenue consists of pay-per-view and advertising. Advertising revenue is given by $R_a = 4q_s$ and the demand for televised sport is $p_s = 10 - 0.5q_s$. The cost of the television company, consisting of TV rights and operating costs to broadcast the games, is fixed at $C = 50$. If the TV company is a profit maximiser, will it choose pay-per-view or free-to-air?

3. Player labour market

3.1 INTRODUCTION

The players are the most important labour input in the industry of professional team sports; other important labour inputs are coaches, youth trainers, maintenance workers, managers and so on. In this chapter we only consider the input of playing talent. The peculiar economics of the professional team sports industry has not only inspired league administrators to interfere in the product market but also in the player labour market. Their major concern has always been the competitive balance in the league. The argument goes that a competitive player market will lead to a concentration of all playing talents in the rich large-market clubs. A rich club can afford to offer the best players a higher salary and, if they are free to move, the best players will play for the best paying teams. This will result in a championship with a low uncertainty of outcome. Another concern has been the bidding up of top player salaries in the clubs' rat race for the best players in a competitive market, which can cause serious financial problems in many clubs.

In the past, the most important league regulation of the player market has been the restriction on the free movement of players. The so-called Reserve Clause in the USA, which was lifted in the mid-seventies, and the so-called (retain and) transfer system in Europe, which was abolished in the mid-nineties, did not allow players to change teams at the end of their contract. The abolition of these restrictions has certainly made the player labour market more competitive. Other regulations have shown up however, which can seriously affect player salaries and the distribution of talent among teams. These include the rookie draft, revenue sharing arrangements and salary caps. In most sections of this chapter, we will study the labour market in terms of the number of playing talents and not the number of players. One obvious reason is that in all team sports the number of players that can be fielded is fixed, or, as in many sports, the league fixes the (maximum) number of players on the roster. Another reason is that players are very heterogeneous; there are top players and there are more moderate players. Top players have many playing talents; moderate players are less talented. In order to have a homogeneous labour input, we deal with playing talents, so the wage rate or the salary level is the unit cost of talent. A player with many talents is better paid and costs more than a player with few talents. This approach has its disadvantages as well, apart from the fact that the empirical implementation is problematic. The same number of playing talents in a team and on the roster can hide a totally different playing strength. In one football team with 11 players, 100 talents might be equally divided over the 25 players on the roster so that each player only has 4 talents; another club might also have 100 talents, but the 11 best players together have 66 talents. The latter team can be 50 per cent stronger than the former, which only has 44 talents in any team of 11 players that it fields.

In this chapter, the functioning of the player market will be investigated, in both a profit- and a win-maximisation scenario. After a discussion of demand and supply in the talent market, we will analyse different models based on different assumptions regarding the supply of talent.

3.2 DEMAND AND SUPPLY IN THE TALENT MARKET

From microeconomic theory, we know that the market supply curve of labour is an upward-sloping function of the wage rate and, as in most labour markets of highly-skilled workers, the short-term wage elasticity of labour supply is very low. Because professional players are highly skilled and well trained, we can make the simplifying assumption, without much loss of generality, that in a league with a closed labour market, the supply of talent is constant in the short run. The player markets of the North American major leagues can be considered as closed markets. The national football leagues of most European countries, however, are operating in an open EU player market since the abolition of the transfer system by the Bosman verdict (European Court of Justice, 1995). This market cannot be approached by a fixed-supply model because clubs can hire talents from other countries, even mid-season, which changes the supply of talent in the national leagues.

We also know from microeconomic theory that the demand for talent of a profit-maximising firm is given by the marginal revenue. The season revenue function of a club that is concave in the winning percentage, was defined in (2.4) as:

$$R_i = R_i[m_i, w_i, p_i] \tag{3.1}$$

We have already assumed that the market size of a club is not a decision variable. Also, the winning percentage of a team cannot be controlled by the team owner. Although he can try to increase his team's winning percentage by hiring more talents, he has no full control of it because it also depends on the playing strength of the other teams in the league. We therefore need to specify the relationship between the winning percentage and the number of talents.

Borghans and Groot (2005) have derived the relationship between the season winning percentage and the talents of a team by starting from the winning percentage of a team in an individual game:

$$w_{ij} = \frac{t_i}{t_i + t_j}$$

where t_i and t_j are the number of talents of the teams (not the number of players!), and w_{ij} is the probability that team i will win the game against team j. If there are n teams in the league and each team plays $n-1$ games, the expected number of wins is:

$$g_{wi} = \sum_{j \neq i}^{n} \frac{t_i}{t_i + t_j}$$

The (expected) winning percentage is then:

$$w_i = \frac{g_{wi}}{n-1} = \frac{1}{n-1} \sum_{j \neq i}^{n} \frac{t_i}{t_i + t_j} \tag{3.2}$$

From this relationship one can derive that the sum of the winning percentages equals $n/2$. Although this relationship between winning percentage and talent is correct, it considerably complicates the derivation of the marginal revenue of talent. We therefore choose the following simple approximation of the winning percentage:

$$w_i = \frac{n}{2} \frac{t_i}{\sum_j^n t_j} \tag{3.3}$$

The winning percentage of a team is $n/2$ times the ratio of its talents to all talents in the league. Although the sum of these winning percentages is also equal to $n/2$, there is an important difference between the two measures. The ratio of the winning percentages of any two teams, based on (3.3), is the same as the ratio of the talents:

$$\frac{w_i}{w_j} = \frac{t_i}{t_j} \qquad \text{for all } i \text{ and } j,$$

which is clearly not true for relationship (3.2). Only in the special case of a two-team league are both expressions identical. Another disadvantage of this simplification is that the winning percentage can be larger than one if a team holds more than $2/n$ per cent of total league talent.

Continuing with relationship (3.3), the marginal revenue of talent, which is also a decreasing function of talent, can be calculated. A club owner who wants to maximise his profits, will hire talents until the marginal revenue of talent is equal to the marginal cost of talent. The marginal revenue of talent is:

$$\frac{\partial R_i}{\partial t_i} = \frac{\partial R_i}{\partial w_i} \frac{\partial w_i}{\partial t_i}$$

where:

$$\frac{\partial w_i}{\partial t_i} = \frac{n}{2} \frac{\sum_{j=1}^{n} t_j - t_i \left(1 + \sum_{j \neq i}^{n} \frac{\partial t_j}{\partial t_i}\right)}{\left(\sum_{j=1}^{n} t_j\right)^2}. \tag{3.4}$$

This expression needs a closer look. If the talent market is competitive and market demand always equals market supply by the adjustment of the flexible price of talent, the total sum of talents in the denominator of (3.3) equals the total supply of talent. If this supply of talent is fixed, and, assuming perfect information, team owners are aware of the fact that hiring one more talent implies an equal loss of talent in another team, that is, $\sum_{j \neq i}^{n}(\partial t_j/\partial t_i) = -1$; they take this information into account when calculating the marginal revenue of talent. It follows that (3.4) simplifies to:

$$\frac{\partial w_i}{\partial t_i} = \frac{n}{2s} \tag{3.5}$$

where s is the fixed talent supply. Because $n/2s$ is a constant, it can be normalised to equal one so that the marginal revenue of talent is equal to the marginal revenue of winning. So, by the internalisation of the talent supply, the winning percentage in revenue function (3.1) can simply be replaced by the number of talents. By this substitution, however, the demand for talent of one team is not affected by the hiring strategies of the other teams in the league, so a club owner has full control of the season winning percentage of his team (see Quirk and Fort, 1992; Vrooman, 1995). Under these assumptions, each profit-maximising club determines its downward-sloping demand curve for talent by equalising marginal revenue and marginal cost of talent. The sum of the clubs' demand curves yields the market demand curve for talent and the market mechanism fixes the equilibrium unit cost of talent. This is the well-known Walras equilibrium model applied to the player labour market.

This approach has recently been criticised by Szymanski and Késenne (2004). They argued that the internalisation of the fixed talent supply is questionable, and that a Nash equilibrium model rather than a Walras equilibrium model should be used to analyse the player labour market. In the rat race for the best players, it seems reasonable to assume that, with a relatively limited number of teams in a league, clubs will react to the hiring strategies of their opponents in the league, so a game theoretic approach is more appropriate.

Taking things step by step, we will first analyse the player labour market using the fixed-supply Walras equilibrium model in section 3.3. Section 3.4 presents the Nash equilibrium model with a flexible talent supply, on the one hand, and a fixed talent supply that is not internalised by the owners, on the other hand. In order to concentrate on the labour market issues, we assume in all models of Chapter 3 that the ticket price is fixed.

3.3   WALRAS EQUILIBRIUM MODEL

As discussed above, if the supply of talent is fixed and internalised in the hiring decisions of all club owners, the winning percentage in revenue function (3.1) can simply be replaced by the number of talents. Because one of the conditions was that the right-hand side of (3.5) is normalised to equal one, it implies also that the sum of talents has to equal $n/2$.

Leaving out the fixed ticket price, the revenue function of each team, based on the assumptions on the impact of market size and playing talent in (2.5), can now be simplified to:

$$R_i = R_i[m_i, t_i] \qquad \frac{\partial R_i}{\partial m_i} > 0 \quad \frac{\partial R_i}{\partial t_i} > \text{or} < 0 \quad \frac{\partial^2 R_i}{\partial t_i^2} < 0 \quad \frac{\partial^2 R_i}{\partial t_i \partial m_i} > 0 \qquad (3.6)$$

Each team's cost function is still:

$$C_i = ct_i + c_i^0.$$

With these specifications, the market outcome in a profit- and a win-maximisation league will be analysed.

3.3.1 Profit Maximisation

In a competitive player market where all clubs are profit maximisers, the market equilibrium can be found where the marginal revenue of talent of each club is equal to the marginal cost, which is the equilibrium unit cost of talent c:

$$MR_i = \frac{\partial R_i[m_i, t_i]}{\partial t_i} = c \quad \text{for all } i: 1, n.$$

If no further assumptions are made regarding the specification of the revenue function beyond concavity, it is possible that a club in a large market with a large drawing potential for players and spectators will hire fewer talents than a club with a small drawing potential. This is not very realistic, and it is also not a very relevant starting point for the derivation of further analytical results. The revenue functions one starts from should be 'well-behaved' in the sense that, for any given marginal cost of talent, a club in a large market hires more talents than a club in a small market. A specification that fulfils this condition, and also considerably simplifies the analysis, is the following quadratic revenue function:

$$R_i = m_i t_i - \beta t_i^2 \quad \text{for } i: 1, n$$

with a marginal revenue of talent that is linear in talent

$$\frac{\partial R_i}{\partial t_i} = m_i - 2\beta t_i.$$

However, one should be aware that all results derived from this revenue function do not necessarily hold for more general revenue functions (see Fort and Quirk, 2004). The market equilibrium can now be found by setting the marginal revenues of all clubs equal to the market-clearing unit cost of talent:

$$m_i - 2\beta t_i = c \quad \text{for all } i,$$

so the demand for talent of each club can be written as:

$$t_i^\pi = \frac{m_i - c}{2\beta}. \tag{3.7}$$

This result indicates that the size of the market increases the demand for talent and that the salary level reduces the demand. Given that the supply of talent is constant and, according to (3.5), equal to half the number of teams, $s = \sum_{i=1}^{n} t_i = n/2$, we can find the market-clearing salary level in a competitive player market where market demand equals market supply:

$$\frac{\sum_{i=1}^{n} m_i - nc}{2\beta} = s = \frac{n}{2} \qquad \text{so that} \qquad c^\pi = \overline{m} - \frac{2\beta s}{n} = \overline{m} - \beta.$$

From this solution one can see that the supply of talent has a negative effect, and that the average market size, affecting the demand for talent, has a positive effect on the salary level. (In order to yield positive values for talent demand and salary level, it is necessary that $\overline{m} - m_i < \beta < \overline{m}$.)

By substituting the salary level in expression (3.7) the number of talents hired by all clubs can be found as:

$$t_i^\pi = \frac{1}{2} + \frac{m_i - \overline{m}}{2\beta} \tag{3.8}$$

So it is clear that the club with the largest market also has the largest number of talents. This market equilibrium, under perfectly competitive conditions, is Pareto-optimal in the sense that all talents are efficiently allocated over the teams so that total league revenue is maximised.

To illustrate this market equilibrium graphically, let us assume that there are only two clubs in the league, a large-market club x and a small-market club y, and that both clubs only differ in the size of their markets. The equilibrium can be seen in Figure 3.1. On the vertical axis the unit cost of talent is indicated, and on the horizontal axis the number of playing talents. The origin of the large-market club is on the left side of the diagram, the origin of the small-market club is on the right side. The distance between the two origins indicates the constant supply of playing talent. Both clubs have a downward-sloping demand curve or marginal revenue curve (MR), but because the market of club x is larger than the market of club y, the demand for talent of club x, for a given salary level, is higher than the demand of club y. The points of intersection with the vertical axes are equal to the market sizes. The slopes of the two demand curves are equal and given by the parameter β. The player market equilibrium can then be found at point E^π where the two demand curves intersect, because at this point, the sum of the talent demands of both clubs equals the talent supply.

The equilibrium salary level or unit cost of talent is c^π. If the salary level is higher than c^π, one can see in Figure 3.1 that total demand for talent is lower than total supply, so the flexible player salary will decrease. If the salary level is lower than the equilibrium value, total demand is higher than

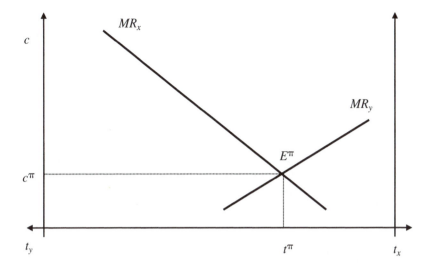

Figure 3.1   Profit maximisation

total supply, so the player salary level will increase. In the equilibrium point, the distribution of playing talent between both clubs can be seen on the horizontal axis. What this figure shows is that, at the market equilibrium, the large-market club has more talents than the small-market club (see Quirk and Fort, 1992).

3.3.2   Comparing Profit and Win Maximisation

In Chapter 1, we have already mentioned that different club objectives can be expected to have a different impact on the number of talents hired by a club. In this section we will investigate what difference it makes in a Walras equilibrium model if all clubs in a league are win maximisers. Given the specifications of the model, the only way club owners can maximise the team's winning percentage is by hiring as many talents as they can afford given the limits of their budget. So, the decision model can also be written as:

$$\max t_i \quad \text{subject to:} \quad R_i[m_i, t_i] - ct_i - c_i^0 = \pi_i^0$$

where π_i^0 is a fixed amount of season profits. To start with the simplest model, we assume that the capital cost is zero, $c_i^0 = 0$, and that club owners are not interested in making profits, so the number of talents is maximised under the breakeven constraint, $\pi_i^0 = 0$. It follows that a club spends all its revenue on talent. Under these hypotheses, and using the Lagrange function, the first-order conditions for win maximisation can then be written as:

$$1 + \lambda_i \left(\frac{\partial R_i}{\partial t_i} - c \right) = 0$$

$$R_i - ct_i = 0$$

where λ_i is the positive Lagrange multiplier. From the first equation, it can be seen that $MR_i = c - 1/\lambda_i < c$, so the marginal revenue from talent is smaller than the marginal cost. It follows that the demand for talent, for a given unit cost of talent, is higher if a club is a win maximiser rather than a profit maximiser.

The second equation shows that a club's demand curve for talent is not given by the marginal revenue curve but by the average revenue curve, which is the revenue per unit of talent, or $R_i/t_i = AR_i = c$. This can also be shown graphically. If the marginal revenue is higher than the average revenue, the average revenue increases. If the marginal revenue is lower than the average revenue, the average revenue decreases. It follows that the marginal revenue curve runs through the maximum point of the average revenue curve. So, in the relevant downward-sloping part of the average revenue curve, the marginal revenue curve is below the average revenue curve and also steeper than the average revenue curve. This can be seen in Figure 3.2. For a given salary level or unit cost of talent c^*, a profit maximiser is hiring t^π talents and a win maximiser is hiring t^w talents.

The competitive market equilibrium in a win-maximisation league can then be found by solving:

$$AR_i = \frac{R_i[m_i, t_i]}{t_i} = c \qquad \text{for all } i\text{: } 1, n.$$

With a quadratic revenue function as specified above, the average revenue curve is also linear, but with a slope that is half the slope of the marginal revenue curves:

$$AR_i = m_i - \beta t_i \qquad \text{for } i\text{: } 1, n.$$

A first implication of win maximisation is a higher demand for talent, given a certain salary level:

$$t_i^w = \frac{m_i - c}{\beta} \qquad \text{so} \qquad t_i^w > t_i^\pi.$$

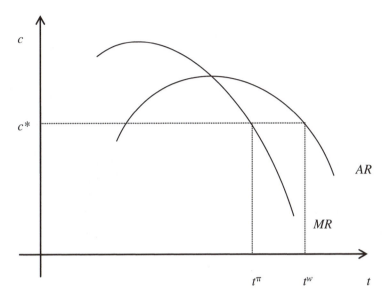

Figure 3.2   Marginal (MR) and average revenue (AR)

A second implication is that, given the same talent supply, the equilibrium salary level will be higher than in a profit-maximisation league. Players in a win-maximisation league are paid above the value of their marginal revenue. The salary level can again be found by equalising the market demand for talent and the constant market supply of talent:

$$c^w = \frac{2\sum_{i=1}^{n} m_i - n\beta}{2n} = \overline{m} - \frac{\beta}{2} \qquad \text{so} \qquad c^w > c^\pi.$$

A third implication is that the distribution of talent among clubs is more unequal if the clubs' objective is to win rather than to make profits. The talents hired by the clubs can be calculated as:

$$t_i^w = \frac{1}{2} + \frac{m_i - \overline{m}}{\beta} \tag{3.9}$$

so the difference between the hiring of talents in both leagues is:

$$t_i^w - t_i^\pi = \frac{m_i - \overline{m}}{2\beta}$$

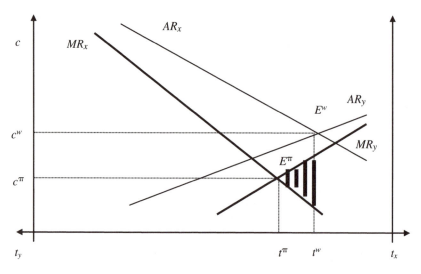

Figure 3.3   Win versus profit maximisation

A large-market club in a win-maximisation league has more talents than the same large-market club in a profit-maximisation league, and a small-market club in a win-maximisation league has fewer talents than the same small-market club in a profit-maximisation league. It follows that the competition is more unbalanced in a win-maximisation league than in a profit-maximisation league. This can also be seen by substituting m_i from (3.8) into (3.9), so it can be derived that:

$$t_i^w = 2t_i^\pi - 0.5.$$

Using the standard deviation as an indicator of the talent distribution, it is clear that the standard deviation of t_i^w is twice the standard deviation of t_i^π.

A fourth implication is that, in a win-maximisation league, total league revenue is lower than in a profit-maximisation league. By moving away from the profit-maximisation equilibrium, playing talent is no longer efficiently allocated over clubs. Some players are not playing in the team where their marginal revenue is at the highest possible level.

The competitive balance in both scenarios can be seen in Figure 3.3, which shows the demand curves for talent under both the profit- and the win-maximisation hypotheses. The point of intersection of the two MR curves yields the market equilibrium (E^π) in a profit-maximisation league, with a distribution of talent (t^π), and the market-clearing unit cost of playing talent (c^π). The talent demand functions under win-maximisation are given by the AR curves. Their point of intersection indicates the market equilibrium in a win-maximisation league (E^w). As can be seen, the distribution of talent in a win-maximisation league (t^w) is more unequal, and the unit cost of playing talent is higher ($c^w > c^\pi$). Moreover, under win maximisation all talents between the points t^π and t^w are playing in the large-market team, where their marginal revenue is lower than in the small-market team. This misallocation of talent in a win-maximisation league is causing a loss of league revenue, which can be measured by the hatched area. By moving from E^π to E^w, the gain in total revenue of the large-market club is offset by the loss in total revenue of the small-market club.

The special case of a two-club model
In a simplified model where there are only two clubs in a league, the market equilibrium under **profit maximisation** can be found by equalising the marginal revenues of both clubs:

$$m_x - 2\beta t_x = m_y - 2\beta t_y$$

where $m_x > m_y$. With a constant supply of talent equal to one, $t_x + t_y = 1$, we can find the talents hired by both clubs:

$$t_x^\pi = \frac{1}{2} + \frac{m_x - m_y}{4\beta} \quad \text{and} \quad t_y^\pi = \frac{1}{2} - \frac{m_x - m_y}{4\beta}.$$

The competitive balance in the league, or the distribution of talents, can now be indicated by the difference between the talents:

$$t_x^\pi - t_y^\pi = \frac{(m_x - m_y)}{2\beta},$$

which shows that the large-market team has the highest number of talents. The equilibrium salary level can be found by equalising the market demand for talent, which is the sum of the demand curves of both clubs, and the market supply of talent:

$$\frac{m_x - c^\pi}{2\beta} + \frac{m_y - c^\pi}{2\beta} = 1 \quad \text{so:} \quad c^\pi = \frac{m_x + m_y - 2\beta}{2} = \overline{m} - \beta.$$

Under **win maximisation**, the player market equilibrium can be found by equalising the average revenues of both clubs:

$$m_x - \beta t_x = m_y - \beta t_y.$$

The hiring of talent is then:

$$t_x^w = \frac{1}{2} + \frac{m_x - m_y}{2\beta} \quad \text{and} \quad t_y^w = \frac{1}{2} - \frac{m_x - m_y}{2\beta}.$$

The competitive balance can then be written as:

$$t_x^w - t_y^w = \frac{(m_x - m_y)}{\beta},$$

which is clearly more unequal than under profit maximisation.

The salary level can again be found by setting the market demand for talent equal to the constant market supply of talent so that:

$$c^w = \frac{m_x + m_y - \beta}{2} = \bar{m} - \frac{\beta}{2}.$$

In a win-maximisation league, players are better paid because the demand for talent is higher. The loss of total league revenue in a win-maximisation league, due to the inefficient allocation of talent, can then be found as:

$$R^\pi - R^w = \frac{(m_x - m_y)^2}{8\beta}.$$

Remarks

1. Fort and Quirk (2004) have shown that nothing can be derived regarding the competitive balance in a win-maximisation league compared with a profit-maximisation league if no simplifying assumptions are made about the revenue functions beyond concavity. We have seen above that, if we just assume that revenue functions are concave in talent, we find the very unlikely result that, all else being equal, the small-market club hires more talents than the large-market club. This can even occur in a two-club model with simple quadratic revenue functions by allowing the parameter β to be different in the large- and the small-market club:

$$R_i = m_i t_i - \beta_i t_i^2 \quad \text{for } i = x, y \quad \text{and} \quad m_x > m_y. \tag{3.10}$$

One can derive that in this case a win-maximisation league can yield a more equal talent distribution than a profit-maximisation league. However, this will only occur in the rather unrealistic scenario that the small-market team hires more talents than the large-market team (see

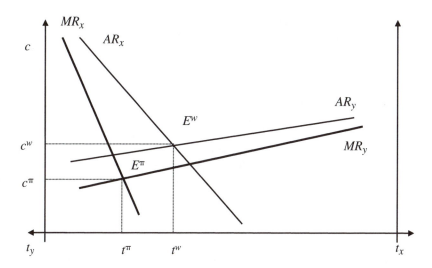

Figure 3.4   When a rich club has a poor team

also Vrooman, 1995). In a profit-maximisation league the condition is that:

$$\beta_x - \beta_y > m_x - m_y.$$

In a win-maximisation league the condition is that:

$$\beta_x - \beta_y > 2(m_x - m_y)$$

in other words, if the difference between the slopes of the demand curves is larger than twice the difference between the market sizes.

This scenario is shown in Figure 3.4. Although club x has a larger market than club y, which is indicated by the starting points of the demand curves on the vertical axis, the large-market club is less talented because of the differences in the slopes of the demand curves. One can see that in this case the competitive balance is more unequal in the profit-maximisation league.

To avoid this unlikely outcome, we have assumed that the parameter β, which is the slope of the demand curve, is the same for every club. This is a sufficient, but not a necessary condition for the quadratic revenue function to be well-behaved, that is, to guarantee that, all else being equal, the team with the largest market club has the highest number of talents. One could argue that the value of the parameter β

should be different for each club, because it should depend on market size: the larger the market, the larger the value of β. The reason is that for each team the marginal revenue of winning should approach zero if the winning percentage approaches unity:

$$m_i - 2\beta_i = 0 \quad \text{for all } i \qquad \text{so: } \beta_i = m_i/2 \quad \text{for all } i \neq j.$$

For simplicity reasons, however, and because it does not change the most fundamental results, we accept the same slope for every club.

2. Another question is whether the conclusions that we have derived so far also hold for other well-behaved specifications. One functional form that comes to mind is the well-known Cobb–Douglas specification:

$$R_i = m_i^\alpha t_i^\beta \quad \text{for } i = x, y \quad \text{with} \quad 0 < \alpha < 1 \quad \text{and} \quad 0 < \beta < 1.$$

One can derive that this specification is well-behaved: the profit-maximising large-market club hires more talents than the small-market club:

$$\frac{t_x}{t_y} = (m_x^\alpha/m_y^\alpha)^{\beta-1} > 1.$$

However, as indicated by Dobson and Goddard (2001), the talent distribution for win-maximising clubs turns out to be exactly the same. Does it mean that one of the conclusions above, namely that the competitive balance in a win-maximisation league is more unequal than in a profit-maximisation league, is not generally true for well-behaved revenue functions? In fact, one has to add at least one more condition regarding the specification of the revenue function, in order to make it well-behaved for the sports industry. The diminishing effect of the winning percentage on the marginal revenue must be stronger, the more a team's winning percentage approaches 100 per cent. This implies that the third-order partial derivative of the revenue function with respect to the winning percentage, or the number of talents, should be negative, or zero at the most, but certainly not positive as it is in the Cobb–Douglas function. In the graphical presentation of Figure 3.1, it means that the marginal revenue curves should be concave to the origin or linear. The Cobb–Douglas specification does not fulfil this condition, so it is not a suitable revenue function for professional sports clubs.

3. We can relax the assumption of a zero-capital cost and/or a zero profit rate. Starting from the club's budget constraint $R_i = ct_i + c_i^0 + \pi_i^0$, the demand curves for talent are the net-average revenue curves:

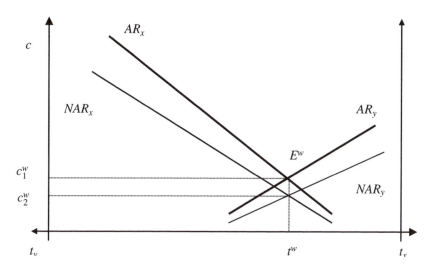

Figure 3.5   Average revenue (AR) and net average revenue (NAR)

$$NAR_i = \frac{R_i - c_i^0 - \pi_i^0}{t_i}$$

If the capital cost of a large-market club is much larger than the capital cost of a small-market club, it is possible that the small-market club may become the more talented one. Moreover, the distribution of talent in a win-maximisation league may be more equal then in a profit-maximisation league. If we assume that the total capital compensation is more-or-less proportional to the club's revenue, $c_i^0 + \pi_i^0 = kR_i$, where k is the proportionality factor, the net average revenue curves become:

$$NAR_i = \frac{(1-k)R_i}{t_i} = (1-k)AR_i.$$

In the two-club model with quadratic revenue functions, the net average revenue curves are again linear, but less steep and below the average revenue curves. These adjustments do not change the competitive balance in a win-maximisation league, but they will lower the player salary level. This is shown in Figure 3.5. Notice that this pro-portionality assumption also shifts the demand curves in a profit-maximisation league.

4.   We can also consider the possibility that, in one league, some clubs are profit maximisers while other clubs are win maximisers, or that the

fixed profit rate of one club is higher than that of another club. If the large-market club is assumed to be more (less) profit orientated than the small-market club, the competitive balance in the league will improve (worsen). This can easily be seen in Figure 3.3, by considering the point of intersection of the marginal revenue curve of club x, being the profit maximiser, and the average revenue curve of club y, being the win maximiser.

5. In his *General Theory of Professional Sport Leagues*, Vrooman (1995), starting from more general revenue and cost functions, such as:

$$R_i = R_0 m_i^\alpha w_i^\beta \quad \text{and} \quad C_i = C_0 m_i^\gamma w_i^\delta,$$

investigated how the competitive balance in a league can also be affected by differences in the revenue elasticity of winning (or talent). If the revenue elasticity of a win (β) is larger for a small-market team, the dominance of the large-market team can be reduced. The competitive balance will also improve if the cost elasticity of winning (δ) increases. Also, the existence of negative cost externalities of market size (γ) can improve the competitive balance.

6. As a last remark, we again consider the club objective function (1.3), which was proposed by Rascher (1997) and which is a linear combination of profits and wins (or talent):

$$\max(R_i - ct_i - c_i^0 + \alpha_i t_i) \quad \text{with } \alpha_i > 0 \qquad \text{for all } i.$$

The talent market equilibrium condition can then be written as:

$$MR_i + \alpha_i = c \quad \text{for all } i.$$

It follows that, for a given unit cost of talent, the demand will be higher than under profit maximisation. Also, the more win orientated clubs are, that is, the larger the value of α_i, the higher the demand for talent will be. It follows that the equilibrium salary level will also be higher. The competitive balance will be the same as under profit maximisation if the value of α_i is the same for all clubs, but differences in the motivation for winning affect the talent distribution. If the small-market clubs are more win orientated, the distribution of talents will be more balanced.

In the two-club model with quadratic revenue functions, the competitive balance can be calculated as:

$$t_x^{\pi w} - t_y^{\pi w} = \frac{m_x - m_y + \alpha_x - \alpha_y}{2\beta}.$$

Even if $m_x > m_y$, the difference between the talent levels can be positive or negative, depending on the α_i values. If the small-market club is much more win orientated than the large-market club, compared with their difference in market size, it is possible that the small-market team dominates the large-market team.

3.3.3 Segmented Player Labour Market

It is well known that some star players in professional team sports are among the best paid workers in the world, making much more money than their grassroot team mates. Some moderate professional players have to play at the minimum wage or are unemployed because they cannot find a team. The extremely high salaries of top athletes can be explained by Rosen's (1981) *Economics of Superstars*, showing that small differences in performance can cause large differences in pay in a winner-take-all competition. The classical example is that of an opera singer: because every opera lover wants to listen to the best tenor in the world, he will sell many more recordings than the second-best tenor. Likewise sports teams fight to hire the top players, and are prepared to pay them skyrocketing salaries, while the sub-top players have to settle for much less.

The model of the player labour market, in terms of the number of talents, cannot deal with this segmentation of the player labour market. In this section, we follow a somewhat different approach, where two types of players are considered: top players and regular players. We start again from a well-behaved club revenue function in market size and winning percentage:

$$R_i = R_i[m_i, w_i] \qquad \text{for all } i. \tag{3.11}$$

We call the number of top players l^T and the number of regular players l^R. The winning percentage of a club depends on the number of top players in the team. We assume that the productivity of a regular player, which is his individual contribution to a club's winning percentage, is only a fraction ε of the productivity of a top player. We can describe this relationship as:

$$w_i = l_i^T + \varepsilon l_i^R \qquad \text{with } 0 < \varepsilon < 1. \tag{3.12}$$

Obviously, a team can only have a fixed number of players L on the field. So, a club faces the restriction that:

$$l_i^T + l_i^R = L \qquad \text{for all } i. \tag{3.13}$$

After the substitution of (3.12) and (3.13) in (3.11), the revenue function can be rewritten as:

$$R_i = R[m_i, \varepsilon L + (1 - \varepsilon) l_i^T] \tag{3.14}$$

On the cost side, we assume that a club's total cost only consists of player salaries. If c^T is the cost or the salary of a top player and c^R is the cost of a regular player, we can write the cost function, given constraint (3.13), as:

$$C_i = (c^T - c^R) l_i^T + c^R L. \tag{3.15}$$

Because the regular players are in excess supply, we assume that their salary is simply a fixed minimum wage. The salary of the top players, however, is determined by demand and supply in the market. We assume that the supply of top players L_s is constant. The optimal number of top players of a profit-maximising club can now be found where the marginal revenue of top players equals the difference between their salary level and the (minimum) salary of the regular players:

$$MR_i^T = (1 - \varepsilon) \frac{\partial R_i}{\partial w_i} = c^T - c^R \quad \text{for all } i.$$

So, the marginal revenue of top players also depends on the difference in player productivity $(1 - \varepsilon)$. Once the number of top players is determined, the number of regular players is given by $l_i^R = L - l_i^T$.

Considering again the two-club model and the quadratic revenue functions, where x is the large-market club and y is the small-market club, the equilibrium on the labour market segment of top players is found where the marginal revenue of both clubs is equal to the salary difference:

$$MR_x^T = c^T - c^R = MR_y^T.$$

Because the market size has a positive effect on the marginal revenue of top players, it follows that the large-market club will hire more top players than the small-market club.

This result can also be seen in Figure 3.6, where the demand curves for top players of the large and the small club intersect at point E. The distribution of top players between the two teams is indicated on the horizontal axis and the salary difference between top and regular players on the vertical axis. The model also shows that the salary difference between the star players and the grassroots players can be very large if there is a limited supply of top players.

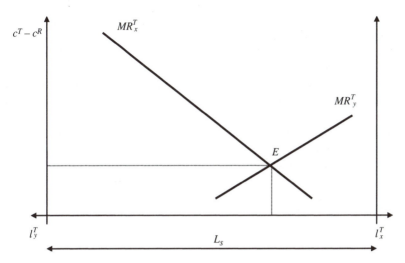

*Figure 3.6   Top players market equilibrium in a profit-maximisation
league*

Because the revenue and cost functions (3.14) and (3.15) are in terms of
the number of top players only, this model is very similar to the model in
terms of playing talents, analysed in the previous sections. So, everything
that has been derived from the model of the player market in terms of
talents can also be interpreted as a model in terms of top players, where the
unit cost of talent can be interpreted as the difference between the top
player salary and the fixed minimum salary of the regular players.

3.4   NASH EQUILIBRIUM MODEL

The Walras equilibrium model in the previous section cannot be used if the
supply of talent is flexible. In the national football leagues in Europe, certainly after the liberalisation of the player labour market by the Bosman
verdict of the European Court of Justice (1995), clubs hire talents from
other national leagues, even in the middle of a season. It follows that an
extra talent in one club does not necessarily imply a loss of talent in another
club in the same league. But even if the supply of talent is fixed, one can
argue that a Nash equilibrium model rather than a Walras equilibrium
model applies. If the talent supply is fixed, strengthening a team by hiring
one more talent has a negative external effect on another team that loses a
talent. In the Walras model, we have assumed that a club takes this externality into account in calculating its marginal revenue, so the externality is

internalised. In a competitive market with perfect information, club owners, in their decisions on talent demand, are assumed to use all the information available. Under these conditions, as discussed in the previous sections, the winning percentage in the revenue function could simply be replaced by the number of playing talents and the hiring strategy of a club would not be affected by the strategies of other clubs. Szymanski and Késenne (2004), however, argue that it is more appropriate, given the relatively limited number of teams in a league, to use a game-theoretic approach because team owners, in their rat race for the best players, will react to the hiring strategies of their opponents. They assert that the internalisation of the external effects is questionable because in that case, given the adding-up condition, one team is left without a choice of strategy.

Starting again from a club's season revenue function $R_i[m_i, w_i]$ with:

$$w_i = \frac{n}{2} \frac{t_i}{\sum\limits_{j}^{n} t_j}$$

the impact of talent on the winning percentage can be derived as in equation (3.4), which is repeated here:

$$\frac{\partial w_i}{\partial t_i} = \frac{n}{2} \frac{\sum\limits_{j=1}^{n} t_j - t_i \left(1 + \sum\limits_{j \neq i}^{n} \frac{\partial t_j}{\partial t_i}\right)}{\left(\sum\limits_{j=1}^{n} t_j\right)^2}$$

If strengthening one team does not lower the talents of the opponent teams in the league, we can no longer assume that $\sum_{j \neq i}^{n}(\partial t_j / \partial t_i) = -1$ as before. Now $\sum_{j \neq i}^{n}(\partial t_j / \partial t_i) = 0$, so the effect of talent on winning is now:

$$\frac{\partial w_i}{\partial t_i} = \frac{n}{2} \frac{\sum\limits_{j \neq i}^{n} t_j}{\left(\sum\limits_{j}^{n} t_j\right)^2} \qquad (3.16)$$

It follows that, when deriving the marginal revenue of talent, one club's hiring of talent depends on the hiring strategies of the other clubs, and a game-theoretic approach is called for. Instead of the Walras equilibrium model, a non-cooperative Nash equilibrium model applies.

In the following two sections, we will discuss the Nash equilibrium under both the profit- and the win-maximisation hypotheses. In a third section, the non-internalised fixed-supply model is investigated. Concerning the unit cost of talent, the usual assumption in a Nash equilibrium approach is that it is exogenously given. An interesting question, however, is how the salary level is determined. One possibility is that all clubs are wage takers on an internationally competitive player market and that the player cost is determined by international demand and supply conditions. It is also possible that salaries are determined by collective bargaining agreements between team owners and players. As is often the case in the US major leagues, players can be united in a player association to counter the monopsony power of teams (see Chapter 5). In this case, the player labour market can be characterised as a bilateral monopoly. As most disputes are on salary levels and profits, the relative bargaining power of players and owners, threatening with player strikes and owner lockouts, will fix the salary levels or, in most cases, the league's salary cap (see Chapter 7). Other possibilities are that team owners pay a win bonus to the players, or unilaterally fix efficiency wages. The latter two cases will be discussed in sections 3.4 and 3.5.

3.4.1 Profit Maximisation

With an exogenous marginal cost of talent c, and assuming profit maximisation, the following reaction functions can be derived for the non-cooperative Nash equilibrium:

$$\frac{\partial R_i}{\partial w_i}\frac{\partial w_i}{\partial t_i} = \frac{\partial R_i}{\partial w_i}\frac{n}{2}\frac{\sum\limits_{j\neq i}^{n} t_j}{\left(\sum\limits_{j}^{n} t_j\right)^2} = c \qquad \text{for all } i. \tag{3.17}$$

The solution of this system of equations yields the Nash equilibrium for the number of talents hired by each club. In a two-team league, this can be written as:

$$\frac{\partial R_x}{\partial w_x}\frac{\partial w_x}{\partial t_x} = \frac{\partial R_y}{\partial w_y}\frac{\partial w_y}{\partial t_y} \quad \text{with} \quad \frac{\partial w_x}{\partial t_x} = \frac{t_y}{(t_x+t_y)^2} \quad \text{and} \quad \frac{\partial w_y}{\partial t_y} = \frac{t_x}{(t_x+t_y)^2},$$

so:

$$\frac{\dfrac{\partial R_x}{\partial w_x}\dfrac{\partial w_y}{\partial t_y}}{\dfrac{\partial R_y}{\partial w_y}\dfrac{\partial w_x}{\partial t_x}} = \frac{t_x}{t_y}.$$

It follows that, if $t_x > t_y$, the marginal revenue of winning is higher in the stronger team than in the weaker team. One implication of this solution is that the Nash equilibrium is inefficient. Total league revenue can be increased by moving talent from the weaker team to the stronger team. In order to reach equality between the marginal revenues of winning, which is the condition for maximum league revenue, the winning percentage of the stronger team has to go up, because club revenue is concave in the winning percentage (see Szymanski and Leach, 2005).

Starting again from a two-club model with quadratic revenue functions in terms of the winning percentage, $R_i = m_i w_i - \beta w_i^2$, the winning percentages simply are:

$$w_x = \frac{t_x}{t_x + t_y} \quad \text{and} \quad w_y = \frac{t_y}{t_x + t_y}.$$

In a profit-maximisation league, the reaction functions of the Nash–Cournot model, applying (3.17), can then be written as:

$$(m_x - 2\beta w_x)w_y = c(t_x + t_y)$$
$$(m_y - 2\beta w_y)w_x = c(t_x + t_y).$$

Equalising the two left-hand sides of the equations yields the following competitive balance:

$$\frac{w_x^\pi}{w_y^\pi} = \frac{m_x}{m_y} \quad \text{with} \quad w_x^\pi = \frac{m_x}{m_x + m_y} \quad \text{and} \quad w_y^\pi = \frac{m_y}{m_x + m_y}$$

or the ratio of the winning percentages is equal to the ratio of the market sizes. This Nash–Cournot model is presented graphically in Figure 3.7. On the horizontal axis, the talents hired by club x are indicated, on the vertical axis the talents of club y. The Nash–Cournot equilibrium is found at the point of intersection A of the two non-linear reaction functions. The competitive balance or the distribution of talents is given by the slope of the line connecting the origin and the equilibrium point.

In this flexible-supply approach, clubs in one league can hire talents from another league. If the absolute quality of the league depends on the number of talents playing, the absolute quality can vary. If the absolute quality is assumed to affect club revenue, the following revenue function can be considered, where absolute quality is measured by the total supply of talent s:

$$R_i = m_i w_i - \beta w_i^2 + \varepsilon_i s \quad \text{for all } i = x, y \quad \text{with } \varepsilon_x > \varepsilon_y.$$

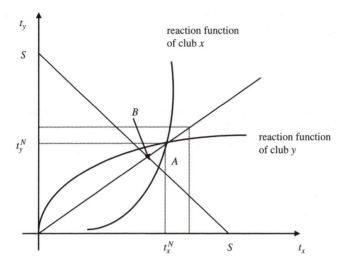

Figure 3.7   Nash–Cournot equilibrium

Solving the reaction equations, one can derive that:

$$m_y w_x - m_x w_y = (\varepsilon_x - \varepsilon_y)(t_x + t_y) > 0, \qquad \text{so:} \quad \frac{w_x^\pi}{w_y^\pi} > \frac{m_x}{m_y}.$$

If the effect of absolute quality on revenue is larger in the large-market club than in the small-market club, the competitive balance turns out to be more unequal than the ratio of the market sizes.

3.4.2   Win Maximisation

For a win-maximising club under the breakeven condition, one can derive from the Lagrange function $w_i + \lambda(R_i - ct_i - c_i^0)$ that:

$$\frac{\partial R_i}{\partial w_i} = \frac{c}{\partial w_i / \partial t_i} - \frac{1}{\lambda_i}$$

where the first term on the right-hand side of the equation is the marginal cost of a win. Because the Lagrange multiplier λ is positive, the marginal cost of a win is now larger than the marginal revenue of a win, as distinct from the profit-maximisation model. It can also be derived from the Lagrange function that the demand for talent is given by the net average revenue, so the reaction functions, with an exogenously given unit cost of talent, can be written as:

$$\frac{R_i - c_i^0}{t_i} = c \qquad \text{for all } i.$$

The solution of this system of equations yields the Nash equilibrium.

For a two-club model with quadratic revenue functions, assuming for simplicity that the compensation of capital (c^0) is zero, the two reaction functions can be written as:

$$\frac{m_x}{t_x + t_y} - \beta\frac{t_x}{(t_x + t_y)^2} = c = \frac{m_y}{t_x + t_y} - \beta\frac{t_y}{(t_x + t_y)^2}.$$

Solving this system of equations simplifies to:

$$m_x - \beta w_x = c = m_y - \beta w_y$$

so the Nash equilibrium yields the following competitive balance:

$$w_x^w - w_y^w = \frac{(m_x - m_y)}{\beta}.$$

It does not come as a surprise that the competitive balance or the distribution of talent is the same in the Nash equilibrium as in the Walras equilibrium. If a team wants to win as much as possible within the limits of its budget, it will spend all its money on talent regardless of the hiring strategy of the other teams in the league.

With the Rascher (1997) objective function, where club owners maximise a linear combination of profits and wins as in (1.3), the reaction functions can be written as:

$$\left(\frac{\partial R_i}{\partial w_i} + \alpha_i\right)\frac{\partial w_i}{\partial t_i} = c \qquad \text{for all } i.$$

For a two-club model, the Nash equilibrium can be found as:

$$\left(\frac{\partial R_x}{\partial w_x} + \alpha_x\right)w_y = \left(\frac{\partial R_y}{\partial w_y} + \alpha_y\right)w_x, \qquad \text{so:} \qquad \frac{w_x^{\pi w}}{w_y^{\pi w}} = \frac{\dfrac{\partial R_x}{\partial w_x} + \alpha_x}{\dfrac{\partial R_y}{\partial w_y} + \alpha_y}$$

The competitive balance is more balanced than under profit-maximisation if the small-market club is more win orientated ($\alpha_y > \alpha_x$).

3.4.3 Fixed Supply of Talent

If the talent supply is fixed, but not internalised as in section 3.3, equation (3.16) can be simplified as:

$$\frac{\partial w_i}{\partial t_i} = \frac{n(s - t_i)}{2s^2}, \qquad \text{thus also:} \qquad \frac{\partial R_i}{\partial t_i} = \frac{\partial R_i}{\partial w_i} \frac{n(s - t_i)}{2s^2} \tag{3.18}$$

where s is the fixed talent supply. It follows that the impact of talent on winning is no longer a constant, so that in revenue function (3.1) the winning percentage can no longer be replaced by the number of talents.

In order to see the implications of this assumption, we consider again a two-club model with quadratic revenue functions. If the fixed talent supply is normalised to equal one, the following demand equations for a **profit-maximising** club can be found, using (3.18):

$$\frac{\partial R_i}{\partial t_i} = (m_i - 2\beta w_i)(1 - t_i) = c, \qquad \text{for } i = x, y. \tag{3.19}$$

These demand functions are no longer linear but quadratic, of the form:

$$2\beta t_i^2 - (m_i + 2\beta)t_i + m_i = c.$$

From (3.19), the competitive market equilibrium can now be derived, which yields the following competitive balance in a two-club model:

$$\frac{w_x^\pi}{w_y^\pi} = \frac{m_x}{m_y} \tag{3.20}$$

The competitive balance is the same as in the flexible-supply model. Comparing this result with (3.7), one can conclude that the competitive balance, or the distribution of talent, is more equal in the Nash equilibrium than in the Walras equilibrium, where the fixed talent supply was internalised:

$$\frac{m_x}{m_y} < \frac{m_x - c}{m_y - c}$$

The explanation is again to be found in the negative external effects that clubs have on each other when hiring new talent. If these externalities are

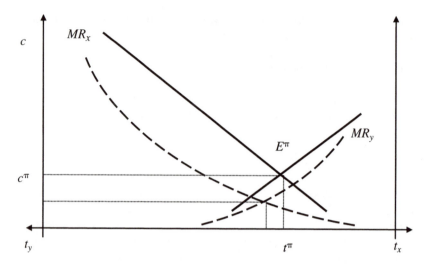

Figure 3.8   Comparing the fixed supply models

fully internalised by club owners in their hiring decisions, the externalities are neutralised. If they are not internalised, and given that the large-market club has a higher marginal revenue than the small-market club, the negative external effects that the small club has on the large club is larger than the negative external effects that the large club has on the small club, so the small-market club is better off (see Szymanski, 2006).

Comparing (3.18) and (3.5), a team's marginal revenue will be lower if the negative external effects of hiring are not internalised. Without internalising the talent losses of the opponents, the team's demand for talent will be lower. It follows that the market-clearing salary level will be lower. This salary level can be calculated by substituting solution (3.20) into the quadratic marginal revenue function (3.19):

$$c^{\pi} = \frac{m_x^2 m_y + m_x m_y^2 - 2\beta m_x m_y}{(m_x + m_y)^2}.$$

In Figure 3.8, the two fixed-supply models are presented and compared graphically. Both the linear and the quadratic demand curves under the profit-maximisation hypothesis are drawn. If the fixed supply of talent is internalised, the linear demand curves intersect at point E^{π}. If the fixed supply of talent is not internalised, the demand curves are non-linear and the point of intersection indicates that the competition is more balanced and the salary level is lower. It follows that this equilibrium does not result in an efficient allocation of talent, because not all available information was taken into account by the team owners.

In Figure 3.7, a constant supply of talent can be represented by a curve *SS*. Given the position of this curve, there is clearly an excess demand for talent in the initial equilibrium point *A*, so in a competitive player market, the unit cost of talent goes up and less talent is hired. The new equilibrium is found in point *B* at the point of intersection of the curve through the origin (representing the competitive balance) and the constant-supply curve *SS*. Thus the competitive balance at point *B* is the same as at point *A*.

If clubs are **win maximisers**, we have to equalise the average revenue curves of the two clubs:

$$\frac{m_x}{t_x + t_y} - \beta\frac{t_x}{(t_x + t_y)^2} = \frac{m_y}{t_x + t_y} - \beta\frac{t_y}{(t_x + t_y)^2},$$

so with a fixed supply of talent normalised to equal one:

$$t_x^w - t_y^w = \frac{m_x - m_y}{\beta} \quad \text{and} \quad c^w = \overline{m} - \frac{\beta}{2},$$

which is again the same result as in the Walras equilibrium model.

Given the results of these Nash equilibrium models for both the flexible- and the fixed-talent supply, the conclusion still stands that the competitive balance will be more unbalanced and that the market-clearing salary level will be higher under win maximisation than under profit maximisation.

3.4.4 Win Bonus

In a sports league, team owners can expect to increase player performances, and the team's winning percentage or profits, by providing a win bonus to the team on top of the players' fixed salary level. In this section, we investigate what the impact of a win bonus is on the winning percentage, the competitive balance, the owner profits and the overall quality in a professional sports league. We extend the two-club model by introducing a simple premium system where a season win bonus is paid on top of a fixed player salary. We consider again profit maximisation and win maximisation. The impact of a premium system can be investigated by introducing a win bonus in just one club. This can also be interpreted as a more generous premium system in one club compared with the premium system in the other club.

If only the small-market club introduces a win bonus, the winning percentages of both the large-market team *x* and the small-market team y, which are a function of their relative number of talents, can be written as:

$$w_x = \frac{t_x}{t_x + et_y} \qquad \text{so:} \qquad \frac{\partial w_x}{\partial t_x} = \frac{et_y}{(t_x + et_y)^2}$$

$$w_y = \frac{et_y}{t_x + et_y} \qquad \text{so:} \qquad \frac{\partial w_y}{\partial t_y} = \frac{et_x}{(t_x + et_y)^2}$$

where e is a index for effort or efficiency. If the effort players are willing to make depends on the win bonus σ, the effort function can be written as

$$e = e[\sigma].$$

Notice that this also implies that the talent ratio is no longer equal to the ratio of the winning percentages:

$$\frac{w_x}{w_y} = \frac{t_x}{et_y}.$$

On the cost side, we assume that the player cost is the only cost of production. Because the large-market club does not introduce a bonus, its cost function is simply $C_x = ct_x$, where c is the exogenously given unit cost of talent. The small-market club's cost, however, consists of a fixed basic salary and a bonus depending on the team's winning percentage at the end of the season. However, it is most likely that the small-market club will decide to pay a lower fixed salary level to make up for the extra cost of the win bonus. Otherwise, players would earn more than the fixed market salary level even if the team only won one game. If the small-market club pays a certain percentage θ of the fixed salary level c, its cost function can be written as:

$$C_y = \theta c t_y + \sigma w_y \qquad 0 \le \theta \le 1 \qquad 0 < \sigma < \frac{\partial R_y}{\partial w_y}.$$

The value of θ is determined in such a way that the players' compensation is the same as without the premium system, i.e.

$$\theta c t_y^0 + \sigma w_y^0 = c t_y^0 \qquad \text{so that} \qquad \theta = 1 - \frac{\sigma w_y^0}{c t_y^0}$$

where w_y^0 and t_y^0 are the win percentage and the talent demand in the benchmark case of no bonus (see Appendix 3.1). We assume that players are motivated to increase effort if their salary depends on the winning percentage. So effort is a positive function of the size of the win bonus σ which is combined with a lower fixed salary level.

$$e = e[\sigma] \quad \text{with} \quad e \geq 1 \quad \frac{\partial e}{\partial \sigma} > 0 \quad e[0] = 1$$

It is important to mention here that there is a lot of uncertainty involved in this model. At the start of the season, when the decision on the size of the win bonus has to be made, club managers do not know what the response of the players and the team's winning percentage will be. They can only rely on an expected value of effort (e) to predict their season revenue and cost. Also, the managers cannot change the number of playing talents of the team during the season, because players are assumed to be under contract for at least one season.

If clubs are **profit maximisers**, the non-cooperative Nash–Cournot equilibrium, given a fixed unit cost of talent, can be found by solving the two reaction equations:

$$\frac{\partial R_x}{\partial w_x} \frac{\partial w_x}{\partial t_x} = c = \frac{1}{\theta} \frac{\partial w_y}{\partial t_y} \left(\frac{\partial R_y}{\partial w_y} - \sigma \right)$$

so:

$$\frac{t_x^{\pi}}{t_y^{\pi}} = \frac{\frac{\partial w_y}{\partial t_y}}{\frac{\partial w_x}{\partial t_x}} \frac{\theta \frac{\partial R_x}{\partial w_x}}{\frac{\partial R_y}{\partial w_y} - \sigma} \quad \text{and} \quad \frac{w_x^{\pi}}{w_y^{\pi}} = \frac{\theta \frac{\partial R_x}{\partial w_x}}{e \left(\frac{\partial R_y}{\partial w_y} - \sigma \right)}.$$

Little can be derived from this general expression because a change in the win bonus also affects effort. We therefore consider a simplified revenue function that is linear in the winning percentage but concave in talent:

$$R_x = \alpha w_x \quad \text{and} \quad R_y = w_y \quad \text{with} \quad \alpha = \frac{m_x}{m_y} > 1.$$

For these revenue functions, it must hold that $0 < \sigma < 1$. The premium system is introduced by the small-market team only. If we want to know the effects of a premium system introduced by the large-market team, or a more generous premium system by the large-market team, we simply have to set $\alpha < 1$.

If both clubs try to maximise profits, the reaction functions can be written as:

$$\frac{\alpha e t_y}{(t_x + e t_y)^2} = c = \frac{e(1 - \sigma)t_x}{\theta(t_x + e t_y)^2},$$

so the Nash–Cournot equilibrium yields the following talent and win ratio:

$$\frac{t_x^\pi}{t_y^\pi} = \alpha \frac{\theta}{1 - \sigma} \qquad \text{and} \qquad \frac{w_x^\pi}{w_y^\pi} = \alpha \frac{\theta}{e(1 - \sigma)}.$$

What can be derived from these solutions? We compare the outcomes with the equilibrium in the benchmark scenario without the premium system where $\theta = 1$, $\sigma = 0$ and $e = 1$, so the talent and win ratio are both equal, $t_x^\pi / t_y^\pi = w_x^\pi / w_y^\pi = \alpha$ (see Appendix 3.1). The talent ratio does not depend on the effort players are willing to make. The winning percentage of the small-market team or the competitive balance is positively affected by the response to the bonus. If the fixed salary level is not reduced ($\theta = 1$), a higher win bonus can improve or worsen the competitive balance, depending on the effort function. A win bonus on top of the full salary level will increase the small-market club's total cost, but it can also increase the club's revenue if the response to the bonus is strong enough, that is, if $e > 1/(1 - \sigma)$. If a positive value of the win bonus is combined with a lower fixed salary ($\theta < 1$), the impact depends on the relative values of the parameters. If $\theta < e(1 - \sigma)$, the competitive balance improves compared with the benchmark.

Since teams are profit maximisers, we want to know the impact of the premium system on profits. To calculate the team's cost, we need the number of talents that are hired by each club:

$$t_x^\pi = \frac{\alpha^2 \theta e(1 - \sigma)}{c\{\alpha\theta + e(1 - \sigma)\}^2}$$

$$t_y^\pi = \frac{\alpha e(1 - \sigma)^2}{c\{\alpha\theta + e(1 - \sigma)\}^2}$$

so, although the talent ratio was not affected, the number of talents of each club is affected by the team's effort. The team's profits can then be calculated as:

$$\pi_x = \frac{\alpha^3 \theta^2}{\{\alpha\theta + e(1 - \sigma)\}^2}$$

$$\pi_y = \frac{e^2(1 - \sigma)^3}{\{\alpha\theta + e(1 - \sigma)\}^2}$$

Table 3.1   Simulation results, profit maximisation

	$\theta = 1$ $\sigma = 0$ $e = 1$	$\theta = 1$ $\sigma = 0.1$ $e = 1.3$	$\theta = 1$ $\sigma = 0.1$ $e^r = 1$	$\theta = 0.85$ $\sigma = 0.1$ $e = 1.3$	$\theta = 0.85$ $\sigma = 0.1$ $e^r = 1$
w_y^π	0.33	0.37	0.31	0.41	0.36
t_x^π	44	47	47	48	48
t_y^π	22	21	21	26	26
Q	66	68	68	74	74
π_x	89	80	91	70	82
π_y	11	12	7	15	10
c_y	1	1.18	1.15	1	0.99

From these profit functions, it can only be derived that a higher win bonus paid by the small-market club will increase the profits of the large-market club ($\partial \pi_x / \partial \sigma > 0$) and that a higher fixed salary level paid by the small-market club will lower its profits ($\partial \pi_y / \partial \theta < 0$).

Because it is difficult to derive the combined impact of a change in two or more parameters, we look at a few results from a simple simulation exercise. In Table 3.1, calculations are made for different values of the fixed salary and the bonus parameter. We assume that the market of the big club is twice as large as the market of the small club ($\alpha = 2$). The exogenously given salary level is normalised to equal one ($c = 1$). The first column presents the benchmark case where no win bonus is paid. In the second column, where the fixed salary is not reduced but a win bonus of 10 per cent is paid by the small-market club, which enhances the team's effort by 30 per cent, so that $e(1 - \sigma) > \theta = 1$, the winning percentage of the small-market club goes up. The small club hires fewer talents but they are more efficient. The large club increases talent demand and the total talents in the league are higher; this can be seen as a measure of the absolute quality of the league (Q). Profits of the large club are down, but the small club's profits go up because its revenue increases more than its player cost. The unit cost of talent in the small-market club (c_y), or the player's compensation, is 18 per cent higher than in the large-market club.

As mentioned before, the team managers can only rely on the expected value of the effort at the start of the season when the players are given a season contract. If the number of talents cannot be changed during the season, we look at the results when the team's effort is not enhanced by the win bonus. This is done in the third column. The parameters are the same as in the second column but it is assumed now that there is no realised effort ($e^r = 1$). This obviously worsens the position of the small club considerably.

Winning percentage and profits are down, and only their non-motivated players are happy. It is the large-market club that profits from the premium system introduced by the small-market club.

In the fourth column, the fixed salary level is lowered by 15 per cent with a 10 per cent win bonus. If the bonus increases effort as expected, the competitive balance strongly improves. Also, the quality of the league is up, as well as the profits of the small-market club. The players' compensation stays more-or-less the same as in the large-market club.

However, if the win bonus turns out to be ineffective, we can see in the fifth column that the premium system still improves the competitive balance, but reduces the small-market club's profits compared with the benchmark case. The profits of the large-market club are not as far down as in the case where the bonus was effective. At the end of the season, the player compensation in the small-market club turns out to be lower than in the large-market club.

These results show that a profit-maximising club has the best chance of increasing its profits by introducing a premium system that consists of a win bonus combined with a lower fixed salary level. But there is a risk: the condition is that players are responsive to the bonus, as expected by the manager. If they are not, profits are down. Another risk is that players may run off to another team if their total pay is too low compared with the opponent teams. If a win bonus is paid on top of the full salary level, the response to the bonus must be strong enough for the club to increase its profits.

In a **win maximisation** league, the assumption is that all club owners try to maximise the team's season winning percentage under the breakeven constraint. In that case, the Nash–Cournot equilibrium can be found from:

$$\frac{R_x[m_x, w_x]}{t_x} = c = \frac{1}{\theta} \frac{R_y[m_y, w_y] - \sigma w_y}{t_y}.$$

Because little can be derived from this general solution, we again use the quadratic revenue function $R_i = m_i w_i - w_i^2$. If the small-market club introduces a premium system, the Nash–Cournot equilibrium can be found from:

$$\frac{m_x w_x - w_x^2}{t_x} = \frac{1}{\theta} \frac{(m_y - \sigma) w_y - w_y^2}{t_y}.$$

Multiplying both sides of the equation by $(t_x + e t_y)$, one can derive that:

$$m_x - w_x = \frac{e}{\theta}(m_y - \sigma - w_y) \qquad \text{so:} \qquad w_y^w = \frac{\theta(1 - m_x) - e(\sigma - m_y)}{e + \theta}.$$

Table 3.2   Simulation results, win maximisation

	$\theta=1$ $\sigma=0$ $e=1$	$\theta=1$ $\sigma=0.1$ $e=1.3$	$\theta=1$ $\sigma=0.1$ $e^r=1$	$\theta=0.92$ $\sigma=0.1$ $e=1.3$	$\theta=0.92$ $\sigma=0.1$ $e^r=1$
w_y^w	0.25	0.36	0.20	0.40	0.25
t_w^w (*)	94	87	87	83	83
t_y^w (*)	31	37	37	44	44
Q	125	124	124	127	127
π_x	0	0	9	0	10
π_y	0	0	−13	0	−12
c_y	1.0	1.1	1.05	1.01	0.98

Note: (*) Notice that without profits or losses, $t_x = R_x = C_x$ and that $t_y = R_y - \sigma w_y/\theta$.

A simulation can reveal again what is going on in this scenario. In Table 3.2, it is assumed that the large club's market size is $m_x = 2$ and the small club's market size $m_y = 1.5$. The exogenous unit cost of talent is again equal to one ($c = 1$). In the first column, the results of the scenario without the premium system are given. In the second column, the small-market club pays a win bonus of 10 per cent on top of the full fixed salary, which enhances effort by 30 per cent. This improves the competitive balance, but the total league quality stays more-or-less the same due to the reduction in talent demand by the large-market club. The players of the small club are better off because their pay goes up by 10 per cent.

As can be seen in the third column, things change dramatically for the small-market club if the team's effort has not improved as expected. Its winning percentage goes down, which causes a financial loss. Only the players are still happy with 5 per cent extra pay. The winner is clearly the large-market team with a higher winning percentage and an unexpected profit.

In the fourth column, the fixed salary is reduced to 92 per cent of the large-market club's salary level with the same win bonus and effort as in column 2. This clearly helps the small-market club to reach its objective. The competitive balance improves as well as the quality of the league.

If the players' effort does not react to the win bonus, the fifth column shows that the small-market team still reaches the same winning percentage than without the premium system, but its failing premium system has caused a financial loss. The club will also have to convince its players to stay given their lower salary. As a win maximiser, the large-market club is not well off, although it realises an unexpected profit.

It is also possible that the team that pays the bonus may make a financial loss because the response to the bonus is stronger than expected. This depends, among other things, on the specification of the revenue function. If the winning percentage has only a weak effect on season revenue, the season cost can be increased more than the season revenue, leading to a financial loss. If the actual effort is different from the expected effort, little can be concluded about the final impact of a premium system on profits and wins.

We can conclude that the impact of a premium system set up by a club in professional team sports is quite complex, given the fact that clubs also react to the strategies of other clubs in the league. The team that introduces a premium system, or a stronger premium system than its opponents, can expect to increase its profits or winning percentage by paying a win bonus combined with a reduced fixed salary. A crucial factor, though, is the players' response to the win bonus. If the team's effort is not enhanced enough by the bonus, the team's profits and winning percentage can go down. Also, the effect that an increased winning percentage has on the current season revenue is an important factor (see Késenne, 2006).

3.4.5 Efficiency Wages

Another hypothesis regarding wage determination is that salaries are unilaterally fixed by the owners. If one of the most important objectives of a team is playing success, team managers can be expected to pay higher salaries than the market salary in order to attract the better players (adverse selection model), or to prevent the good players from leaving the club (labour turnover model), or simply to stimulate players to perform. The winning percentage depends not only on the talents of the players, but also on the effort players are willing to make. So, it is worthwhile to investigate what the implications for the behaviour of teams are if the efficiency wage theory is introduced into the model (see Akerlof and Yellen, 1986).

Let us assume that the winning percentage is not only affected by the relative talent of a team but also by an index representing the effort the team is willing to make, where effort is a function of a club's salary level:

$$w_i = f\left[e(c_i) \frac{t_i}{\sum_{j=1}^{n} t_j} \right].$$

The effort function e is an increasing function of the club's salary level with decreasing marginal returns, that is, $e' > 0$, and $e'' < 0$, with primes indicating derivatives, and with a monotonously increasing function f so that the adding-up condition $\sum_{j=1}^{n} w_j = n/2$ is fulfilled. Most efficiency wage models introduce some kind of relative salary level in the effort functions. The argument goes that players are only willing to make an extra effort if their salary level is higher than what they can expect to be paid in another club, or higher than the equilibrium salary level in a competitive player market. This way, c_i can be interpreted as the level of the salary, relative to the market-clearing salary level. In this scenario, club managers have to decide on both the optimal talent level and the optimal salary level.

Under **profit maximisation**, the first-order partial derivatives of the profit function with respect to the salary level and the number of the playing talents have to equal zero:

$$MR_{ci} = \frac{\partial R_i}{\partial c_i} = \frac{\partial R_i}{\partial w_i} f' e' \frac{t_i}{\sum_{j=1}^{n} t_j} = t_i \tag{3.21}$$

$$MR_{xi} = \frac{\partial R_i}{\partial t_i} = \frac{\partial R_i}{\partial w_i} f' e \frac{\sum_{j \neq i}^{n} t_j}{\left(\sum_{j=1}^{n} t_j\right)^2} = c_i. \tag{3.22}$$

By substituting the first equation into the second, a variant of the so-called Solow Condition (Solow, 1979) can be derived, indicating that the wage elasticity of effort is:

$$\varepsilon_i^{\pi} = e' \frac{c_i}{e} = \frac{\sum_{j \neq i}^{n} t_j}{\sum_{j}^{n} t_j} < 1. \tag{3.23}$$

From this solution one can derive that, in the flexible-supply model, profit-maximising clubs are willing to pay higher efficiency wages than profit-maximising clubs in the internalised fixed-supply model, for which one can easily derive that $\varepsilon_i^{\pi} = 1$. This can be illustrated in Figure 3.9, where the salary level is on the horizontal axis and effort on the vertical axis. The point of tangency between the concave effort function and the slope of the line through the origin, indicating the ratio e/c, marks the point where the effort elasticity equals unity. To the right of this point, the effort elasticity is smaller then zero, so the optimal efficiency wage level is higher ($c_2 > c_1$).

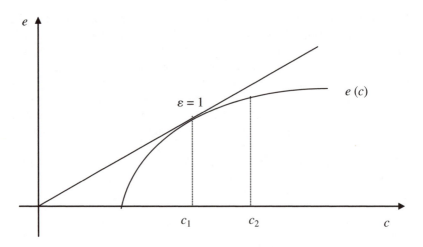

Figure 3.9   Effort function and efficiency wage

Turning to the **win-maximisation** model, the first-order conditions can now be written as:

$$1 + \lambda_i MR_{xi} - \lambda_i c_i = 0$$

$$MR_{ci} - t_i = 0$$

$$R_i[m_i, w_i] - c_i t_i - \pi_i^0 = 0$$

where λ_i is the positive Lagrange multiplier. From the first two equations, the following effort elasticity can be derived:

$$\varepsilon_i^w = \frac{c_i}{c_i - 1/\lambda_i} \frac{\displaystyle\sum_{j \neq i}^{n} t_j}{\displaystyle\sum_{j}^{n} t_j} > \varepsilon_i^\pi \tag{3.24}$$

which is clearly higher than the effort elasticity in a profit-maximising team.

What can be learned from solutions (3.23) and (3.24)? First of all, they can explain why there is unemployment among professional players. One can expect that the optimal and rigid efficiency salary level in a club will be higher than the market-clearing level. The excess supply of talent it causes will not seduce a team owner into lowering the player salary level, because it will lower the efforts his players are willing to make and therefore also the club's profit or the team's winning percentage.

The equations (3.23) and (3.24) also indicate that a club's efficiency wage per unit of talent is set at a higher level the stronger the team is compared with its opponents in the league. So, for a given effort function that is the same for all clubs, the talented clubs are paying higher efficiency wages than the less-talented clubs. This might suggest that efficiency wages set by profit- or win-maximising clubs result in a more balanced competition than equilibrium wages that are determined in a competitive market. If the more talented clubs set higher efficiency wages than the less-talented clubs, one would expect that the demand for talent by the better teams would also be reduced more than the demand of the lesser teams, all else being equal. For at least two reasons, however, little can be derived from this model concerning the competitive balance: first, with efficiency wages there is no longer any guarantee that the demand curves for talent are downward sloping; and second, the relative talent of a club is no longer a reliable indicator of its winning percentage because of the impact of the effort function. Comparing (3.23) with (3.24), one can also see that for a win-maximising club, the effort elasticity is higher, so the efficiency wage is lower. This does not imply that we can expect the efficiency wage in a win-maximisation league to be lower than in a profit-maximisation league. In efficiency wage applications, it is not the absolute salary level that matters, but the salary level relative to a reference level. If this reference level is the market-clearing salary level in a competitive market, we know that this is higher in a win-maximisation than in a profit-maximisation league (see Késenne, 2006).

APPENDIX 3.1   THE BENCHMARK MODEL

The simple model of a two-club league starts from the simplified revenue functions:

$$R_x = \alpha w_x \quad \text{and} \quad R_y = w_y \quad \text{with} \quad \alpha = \frac{m_x}{m_y} > 1,$$

where m is an indicator of the market size and w is the season winning percentage of a team. The winning percentages of a team depend on its relative playing strength, which is captured by:

$$w_x = \frac{t_x}{t_x + t_y} \quad w_y = \frac{t_y}{t_x + t_y}$$

where t stands for a team's number of talents (not the number of players). Considering only the player costs, both club pays an exogenously given salary level c, and the profit functions can be written as:

$$\pi_x = \alpha w_x - ct_x$$
$$\pi_y = w_y - ct_y.$$

Assuming a non-cooperative game, where the two clubs try to maximise their profits, the reaction functions can be written as:

$$\frac{\alpha t_y}{(t_x + t_y)^2} - c = 0$$

$$\frac{t_x}{(t_x + t_y)^2} - c = 0.$$

So the Nash–Cournot equilibrium for the competitive balance or the talent ratio can be found as:

$$\frac{w_x^\pi}{w_y^\pi} = \frac{t_x^\pi}{t_y^\pi} = \alpha > 1.$$

Also, the number of talents hired by each club can be calculated as:

$$t_x^\pi = \frac{\alpha^2}{c(1 + \alpha)^2} \quad \text{and} \quad t_y^\pi = \frac{\alpha}{c(1 + \alpha)^2}$$

$$\text{with} \quad t_x^\pi + t_y^\pi = \frac{\alpha}{c(1 + \alpha)}.$$

The winning percentages are:

$$w_x^\pi = \frac{\alpha}{1+\alpha} \quad \text{and} \quad w_y^\pi = \frac{1}{1+\alpha}.$$

Total revenue and total cost of each club are then:

$$R_x = \alpha w_x = \frac{\alpha^2}{(1+\alpha)} \quad \text{and} \quad R_y = w_y = \frac{1}{(1+\alpha)}$$

$$C_x = ct_x = \frac{\alpha^2}{(1+\alpha)^2} \quad \text{and} \quad C_y = ct_y = \frac{1}{(1+\alpha)^2}$$

so profits are:

$$\pi_x = \frac{\alpha^3}{(1+\alpha)^2} \quad \text{and} \quad \pi_y = \frac{1}{(1+\alpha)^2}.$$

EXERCISES 3

3.1. If the supply of talent is constant, and normalised to equal one, in a Walras equilibrium model with revenue functions $R_x = 160t_x - 100t_x^2$ and $R_y = 120t_y - 100t_y^2$, and if the only cost is the labour cost, what will the distribution of playing talent and the market-clearing unit cost of talent be under profit maximisation? Calculate also the revenues and profits of the large- and the small-market club.

3.2. With the same revenue and cost functions as in exercise 3.1, what will the distribution of playing talent and the market-clearing unit cost of talent be under win maximisation? Calculate the revenues of the large- and the small-market club. Compare these with the profit-maximisation results of exercise 3.1.

3.3. Assume that the competitive balance in a profit-maximisation league with only 6 clubs is given by the following winning percentages w_i^p which add up to 3:

0.70	0.60	0.55	0.50	0.35	0.30

What will the corresponding winning percentages be in a win-maximisation league?

3.4. Use the same revenue and cost functions as in exercise 3.1, but now the large-market club is a profit maximiser and the small-market club is a win maximiser. Calculate the distribution of playing talent and the equilibrium cost of talent.

3.5. With the same revenue and cost functions as in exercise 3.1, but starting from clubs which want to maximise a linear combination of profits and wins, with weights $\alpha_x = 0$ and $\alpha_y = 40$, derive the distribution of talent and the unit cost of talent.

3.6. Start from the same club revenue functions as in exercise 3.1, but assume now that the large-market club faces a fixed capital cost, $c_x^0 = 20$, and that the small-market club's capital cost is zero. Derive the distribution of talent in a win-maximisation league.

3.7. Given the following revenue functions in a two-club model under profit maximisation: $R_x = 160w_x - 100w_x^2$ and $R_x = 120w_x - 100w_x^2$, assume that the players are the only factor of production and that the supply of talent is constant and normalised to equal one. Find the competitive balance and the winning percentages of each club in a Nash equilibrium model. Calculate the equilibrium salary level. Compare the competitive balance and salary level with the flexible-supply Nash equilibrium and the constant-supply Walras equilibrium.

4. Product and labour market

4.1 INTRODUCTION

In this chapter, we analyse ticket pricing, which is one of the important decisions of club owners in the product market, together with talent hiring, which is the most important decision in the labour market. In dealing with the ticket price, we keep the number of talents constant, and in dealing with the demand for talent, the ticket price is fixed. Besides analysing both decisions separately, we also investigate how ticket price and talent demand are connected and how this connection affects the decisions. If the number of talents of a team changes, it will affect its winning percentages and the demand for tickets, so the optimal ticket price is also affected. A change in the ticket price will change attendances and gate receipts, as well as other revenues, so the demand for talent is affected. We therefore develop a two-decision variable model, where club owners have to fix simultaneously, at the start of the season, ticket price and talent demand. We will again compare the solutions under both the profit- and the win-maximisation hypotheses.

4.2 TICKET PRICING AND TALENT HIRING

In this model, most hypotheses made in the previous chapters still hold: clubs are local monopolists and price makers in the product market and wage takers in the player labour market. The supply of talent is fixed and the marginal cost of spectators is zero. The unit cost of a playing talent is determined by demand and supply in a competitive player labour market. Initially, we assume that there are no stadium capacity constraints. Using the Walras equilibrium approach, the season winning percentage in the team's demand function for tickets can be replaced by the number of talents of the team:

$A[m, t, p]$.

The usual assumptions, with subscripts indicating derivatives, hold:

$$A_m > 0 \qquad A_p < 0 \qquad A_t > 0 \qquad A_t = \frac{\partial^2 A}{\partial t^2} < 0. \tag{4.1}$$

However, a few more assumptions are added:

$$A_{tm} = \frac{\partial^2 A}{\partial t \partial m} > 0 \qquad A_{pm} = \frac{\partial^2 A}{\partial p \partial m} > 0 \qquad A_{pt} = \frac{\partial^2 A}{\partial p \partial t} = 0. \qquad (4.2)$$

The first two inequalities state that the impacts of talent and ticket price on attendances are larger for large-market clubs, which is a reasonable assumption. The sign of the last effect is less obvious. Because there seems to be no clear indication for this derivative to be large in a positive or negative sense, we simply assume it to be zero, which means that the demand function is strongly separable into ticket price and talent.

We assume again that all non-gate revenues are proportional to the number of attendances with proportionality factor κ, so the club revenue function can be written as:

$$R = (p + \kappa)A[m,t,p].$$

Also, the club's season cost function is the same as before, consisting of labour and non-labour costs. The capital cost is constant in the short run and, in a competitive player market, the unit cost of a playing talent is the same for all clubs:

$$C = ct + c^0.$$

For a **profit-maximising club**, the first-order conditions are:

$$\pi_p = (p + \kappa)A_p + A = 0 \qquad\qquad\qquad (4.3)$$
$$\pi_t = (p + \kappa)A_t - c = 0 \qquad\qquad\qquad (4.4)$$

The first equation is the well-known pricing rule, showing that the price elasticity is smaller than 1. The second equation indicates that talents are hired until marginal revenue equals marginal cost. The second-order conditions for a maximum require the Hessian matrix to be negative definite, so the following inequalities must hold:

$$\pi_{pp} < 0 \qquad \pi_{tt} < 0 \qquad \pi_{tt}\pi_{pp} - \pi_{pt}^2 > 0 \qquad\qquad (4.5)$$

where:

$$\pi_{tt} = (p + \kappa)A_{tt} < 0$$
$$\pi_{pp} = (p + \kappa)A_{pp} + 2A_p < 0$$

$$\pi_{pt} = \pi_{tp} = (p + \kappa)A_{pt} + A_t = A_t > 0.$$

These conditions can also be illustrated graphically. In Figure 4.1, the two decision variables are found on the axes. From the total differential of the first-order conditions (4.3) and (4.4):

$$d\pi_p = \pi_{pp}dp + \pi_{pt}dt = 0$$

$$d\pi_t = \pi_{tp}dp + \pi_{tt}dt = 0$$

we can find the slopes of the locus $\pi_p = 0$ and $\pi_t = 0$ in the p–t diagram as

$$\frac{dt}{dp}\bigg|_{\pi_p=0} = -\frac{\pi_{pp}}{\pi_{pt}} > 0$$

$$\frac{dt}{dp}\bigg|_{\pi_t=o} = -\frac{\pi_{pt}}{\pi_{tt}} > 0.$$

Given the properties of demand function and the second-order conditions, both slopes are clearly positive. From the second-order conditions, we can also derive that the slope of the locus $\pi_p = 0$ is steeper than the slope of the locus $\pi_t = 0$. The first-order conditions for profit maximisation are met at the point of intersection E^π of the two loci, which marks the optimal price level p_1^π and the optimal number of playing talents t_1^π.

An interesting question is how a rise in player salary affects the optimal ticket price in a two-decision variable model. Remember that we found in Chapter 2 that the optimal ticket price was not affected by the player cost. But in that one-decision-variable model, the hiring of talent was kept constant. In this two-decision-variable model, a club owner has to decide on the hiring of talent as well. From Figure 4.1, we can derive that a higher unit cost of talent will shift the locus $\pi_t = 0$ down, because, for a given price level, talent demand will come down with a higher salary level. It follows that in the new point of intersection, the optimal ticket price p_2^π and talent demand t_2^π are lower. This result can also be derived algebraically. To derive the impact of an exogenous variable on both decision variables, we have to differentiate the first-order conditions (4.3) and (4.4) with respect to the exogenous unit cost of talent c, and solve for $\partial p/\partial c$ and $\partial t/\partial c$:

$$\frac{\partial p}{\partial c} = -\frac{\pi_{pt}}{\pi_{tt}\pi_{pp} - \pi_{pt}^2} < 0$$

$$\frac{\partial t}{\partial c} = \frac{\pi_{pp}}{\pi_{tt}\pi_{pp} - \pi_{pt}^2} < 0.$$

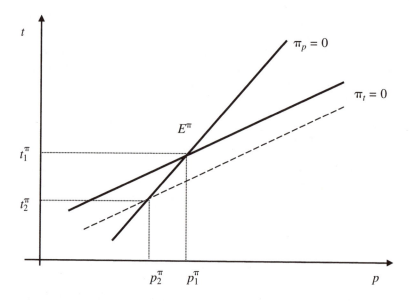

Figure 4.1   Profit-maximising equilibrium

So, contrary to what is generally claimed by many club owners, who argue that player salaries have to be kept low in order to keep ticket prices low, a lower salary level turns out to increase the optimal ticket price set by a profit-maximising owner. Although somewhat counterintuitive, this result can be explained by the fact that a lower salary increases the demand for talent and the winning percentage, which causes the demand curve for tickets to shift to the right, so the profit-maximising ticket price will be set at a higher level. Applying the envelope theorem to the profit function, $\partial\pi/\partial c = -t < 0$, it follows that higher player salaries reduce owner profits, which is probably the real reason why club owners are talking player salaries down.

Comparative static analysis also confirms that large-market clubs hire more talents and charge higher ticket prices than small-market clubs (see Demmert, 1973). In Figure 4.1, a larger value of m would shift the locus $\pi_t = 0$ upward (for a given price, a larger market will increase talent) and the locus $\pi_p = 0$ to the right (for a given talent, a larger market will increase the ticket price), so at the new point of intersection, both the ticket price and the demand for talent are higher.

How does a **win-maximising club** set both ticket price and talent demand at the beginning of the season? If it is the club's objective to maximise the season winning percentage, it hires as many talents as the

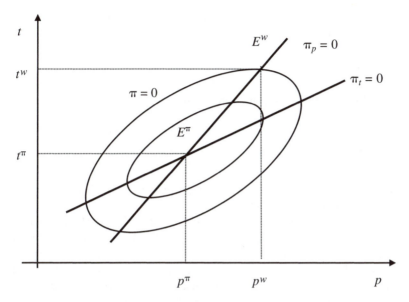

Figure 4.2   Win-maximising equilibrium

budget permits. If the club maximises the number of playing talents under the breakeven constraint, the first-order conditions for win maximisation are:

$$(p + \kappa)A_p + A = 0$$

$$(p + \kappa)A_t = c - \frac{1}{\lambda}$$

$$(p + \kappa)A - ct - c^0 = 0$$

where λ is the positive Lagrange multiplier. The first equation is the pricing rule, which turns out to be exactly the same as under profit maximisation. From the second equation it can be seen that a win-maximising club will hire playing talent up to a point where marginal revenue is lower than marginal cost. The third equation is the budget constraint.

What will the optimal ticket price and talent demand be compared with a profit-maximising club? One way to find out is to look at the iso-profit contours in the p–t diagram. If in Figure 4.2, E^π is the profit-maximising point, it follows that going away from this point in either direction means that profits decrease. The iso-profit contours are now ovals drawn round this point, such that all points on one oval indicate the same profit level. The further away these contours are from E^π, the lower the profits are.

These contours can be found by setting the total differential of the profit function equal to zero:

$$d\pi = \pi_p dp + \pi_t dt = 0,$$

so the slopes of the iso-profit contours are:

$$\left.\frac{dt}{dp}\right|_{d\pi=0} = -\frac{\pi_p}{\pi_t}.$$

It follows that the slopes are zero for all points (p, t) where $\pi_p = 0$, and infinite for all points (p, t) where $\pi_t = 0$.

These iso-profit contours can now be added to the graphical presentation of the first-order conditions in Figure 4.2. The wider these iso-profit contours, and the further away they are from the profit-maximising point, the lower the profits are. One of these contours is the zero-profit contour. If a club maximises the number of talents on the vertical axis, under the breakeven constraint, the equilibrium point is E^w with price p^w and playing talent t^w. It follows that both the demand for playing talent and the ticket price are higher in a win-maximising club than in a profit-maximising club.

4.3   STADIUM CAPACITY CONSTRAINT AND MAXIMUM TICKET PRICE

We derived in Chapter 2 that a club owner, facing a stadium capacity constraint, charges a higher ticket price than without the constraint. The question is whether that is still true if the owner has to decide simultaneously on the hiring of talent. A stadium capacity restriction can be written as:

$$A[m, p, t] \leq A^0$$

where A^0 is the capacity of the stadium. To add this restriction to the p–t diagram, we need to find the inverse demand function and turn it into an equality:

$$t = A^{-1}[m, p, A^0]$$

In this function, the relationship between talent and ticket price is clearly positive because the ticket price has a negative effect on demand, so it has

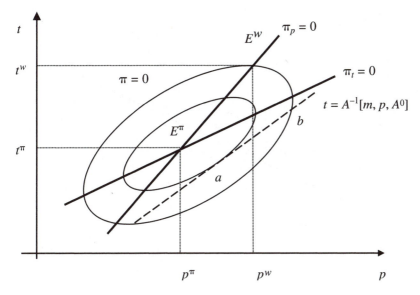

Figure 4.3   Stadium capacity constraint

a positive effect on inverse demand. Given the properties of the ticket
demand function, this restriction is a non-linear convex function.
Nevertheless, there isn't a problem finding a unique point of tangency with
the iso-profit contours (see Késenne and Pauwels, 2006). Therefore the
restriction is simply drawn as a linear curve in Figure 4.3 where only the
points below the curve are feasible. Because the constraint is binding for a
profit-maximising club, its new equilibrium is found at the point of tangency between this restriction and the highest possible iso-profit curve,
which is point *a*. However, the position of that point depends on the slope
of the capacity constraint, and this slope depends on the price and talent
elasticity of the ticket demand function. Therefore, the impact of a stadium
capacity constraint on both the ticket price and the talent demand is theoretically indeterminate.

For a **win-maximising club**, the impact of a capacity constraint is
different. Because there are now two constraints to the maximisation of the
winning percentage, the zero-profit contour and the stadium capacity constraint, the optimal ticket price and talent demand can be found at the
upper point of intersection of the two constraints, which is point *b* in
Figure 4.3. It follows that the demand for talent will be lower under the
capacity constraint. The optimal ticket price can be higher or lower,
depending on the stadium capacity. The more limited the capacity, the
further south-east the curve shifts.

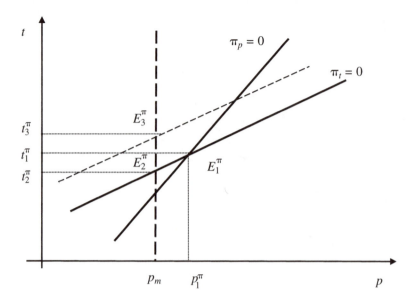

Figure 4.4   Maximum ticket price under profit maximisation

The impact of a maximum ticket price is also more complicated in a two-decision variable model. In Figure 4.4 with first-order conditions $\pi_p = 0$ and $\pi_t = 0$, the **profit-maximising** ticket price and talent demand are determined by the point of intersection E_1^{π}. The maximum ticket price can be represented by the vertical line at the price level p_m. By fixing the price, the locus $\pi_p = 0$ is no longer relevant, so the new optimum is found at the point of intersection E_2^{π} of the vertical p_m line and the locus $\pi_t = 0$. As can be seen, the demand for talent will be lower.

The impact of the maximum ticket price on stadium attendance will depend on the values of the price elasticity and talent elasticity of demand. Even if the total number of spectators in the stadium is not affected, imposing maximum ticket prices can change the composition of the spectators because a lower price will probably attract the more price-elastic low-income people, and a lower winning percentage will discourage the more win-elastic supporters. In any case, owner profits in E_2^{π} will be lower than in E_1^{π}.

So far, we have assumed that the salary level is an exogenously given constant. With an endogenous salary level, a lower demand for talent from all clubs, caused by the maximum ticket price, will also lower the salary level in a competitive player market. A decrease in the salary level causes an upward shift of the locus $\pi_t = 0$, so the impact of imposing a

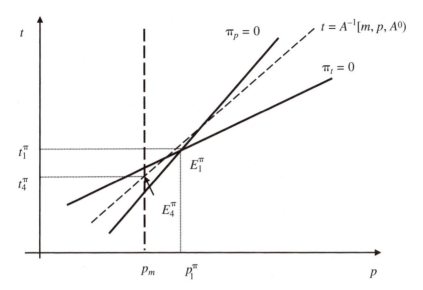

Figure 4.5 *Maximum ticket price and stadium capacity constraint under profit maximisation*

maximum ticket price on the hiring of talent will be theoretically indeterminate. The final effect depends on the level of the maximum ticket price that is imposed, and on the flexibility of the salary level. In Figure 4.4, the case is shown of a relatively large salary decrease, so the final equilibrium point is E_3^π with a higher demand for talent t_3^π. Because attendance and club revenue depend on both ticket price and talent, it is also unclear what the impact of a maximum ticket price is on club revenue, cost and profits.

It is possible that a club's stadium is too small for all spectators who want to attend the games at the lower ticket price. In that case, the club faces two constraints, the maximum ticket price and the stadium capacity. In Figure 4.5, these constraints can be represented by the vertical ticket price line and the stadium capacity constraint. Without the maximum ticket price, the stadium capacity constraint would not be binding, because E_1^π is below the capacity line. With both the maximum ticket price and the stadium capacity constraint, the new equilibrium is found where profits are maximised given these two restrictions, which is clearly at the point of intersection of the two constraints E_4^π.

Ticket price regulations seem even more appropriate if clubs are **win maximisers**. Most clubs are local monopolists on the product market, charging high ticket prices, but win-maximising monopolists will set prices

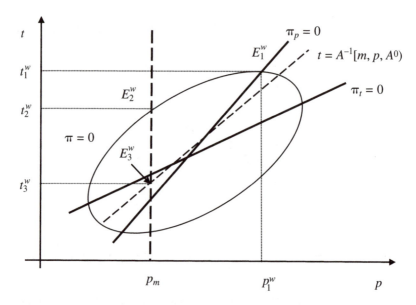

Figure 4.6   Maximum ticket price and stadium capacity constraint under win maximisation

even higher than profit-maximising monopolists. In Figure 4.6 the first-order conditions are drawn again together with the zero-profit contour $\pi=0$. Because a win-maximising club is maximising talent, the equilibrium point is E_1^w. If a maximum ticket price p_m is imposed, the new equilibrium is found at the upper point of intersection E_2^w of the zero-profit contour and the vertical line indicating the maximum ticket price. The result is a lower demand for playing talent. Note that the imposed maximum price can also be too low for the club to stay in business. This happens if the price line is to the left of the zero-profit contour.

If both ticket price and talent demand are coming down, it is again theoretically indeterminate what will happen to attendance. If attendance goes up, but the stadium is too small to accommodate the increased number of spectators, the win-maximising club can choose equilibrium E_3^w at the point of intersection of the ticket price constraint and the stadium capacity constraint. One can see that this implies that the win-maximising club becomes profitable even if that is not an objective. With a decreasing endogenous salary level, the final effect on the demand for talent of imposing a maximum ticket price is again theoretically indeterminate because of the upward shift of the locus $\pi_t = 0$ (see Késenne and Pauwels, 2006).

4.4   NUMERICAL EXAMPLE

A simulation with a simplified model can illustrate some of the results in this chapter. Starting from the following attendance function:

$$A = \{\ln(1 + t) - p\}m$$

the profit function can be written as:

$$\pi = \{p \ln(1 + t) - p^2\}m - ct - c^0.$$

Assuming for simplicity that $m = 1$ and $c^0 = 0$, the first-order conditions for **maximum profits** are:

$$\pi_p = \ln(1 + t) - 2p = 0$$

$$\pi_t = \frac{p}{1 + t} - c = 0$$

which can also be written as:

$$p = \frac{\ln(1 + t)}{2}$$

$$p = c(1 + t).$$

The first relationship between the two decision variables is non-linear, the second is linear. The non-linear and the linear curves clearly have two points of intersection, as can be seen in Figure 4.7, but only one of these points satisfies the second-order condition, where the slope of $\pi_p = 0$ is steeper than the slope of $\pi_t = 0$. Increasing the salary level lowers the slope of the linear curve $\pi_t = 0$ so the optimal ticket price and talent demand are also lower.

Under **win maximisation**, the breakeven condition $p \ln(1 + t) - p^2 - ct = 0$ must hold, so after substituting the pricing rule, $p = \ln(1 + t)/2$ into the budget constraint – this is the same pricing rule as under profit maximisation – one finds that $p = \sqrt{ct}$.

With these equations the model can be solved for profit and win maximisation. In Table 4.1 the simulation results are given for the profit- and the win-maximisation cases and for two different levels of salary, which is the exogenous variable in this model. As can be seen in the first two columns, both the ticket price and the demand for talent are higher in the win-maximisation case. This confirms the results above. For this particular ticket demand function attendance and total revenue are also higher in the

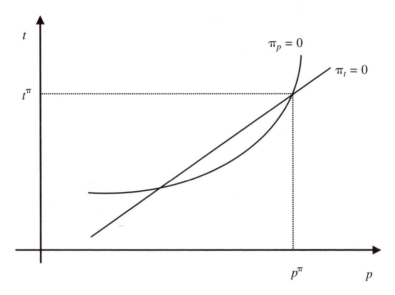

Figure 4.7   First-order conditions for profit maximisation

Table 4.1   Simulation: profit versus win maximisation

	Profit max	Win max	Profit max	Win max	Win max cap =1.0
Salary level	0.08	0.08	0.10	0.10	0.10
Talents	17	50	12	30	20
Ticket price	1.5	2	1.3	1.7	2
Payroll	1.4	4	1.2	3	2
Attendances	1.4	1.9	1.2	1.7	1
Revenue	2.1	4	1.6	3	2
Profits	0.7	0	0.4	0	0

win-maximisation case. The third and the fourth column show that a higher salary level is causing a lower optimal ticket price in both scenarios. It also reduces attendance, revenue, cost and profit for this particular revenue function, but this is not necessarily true for a more general specification of the revenue function.

In the last column, it is assumed that the stadium capacity constraint is 1 for the win-maximising club with the exogenous salary level equal to 0.10. This constraint clearly lowers the talent demand as derived above. For this particular model specification, it also increases the ticket price.

EXERCISES 4

4.1. Assume that the profit function in a two-decision-variable model can be written as:

$$\pi = \frac{p\sqrt{t}}{2} - t$$

calculate the profit-maximising ticket price and talent demand. What will the optimal number of talents be if a maximum ticket price of 6 Euro is imposed by the league?

4.2. Assume that the ticket demand function of a win-maximising club is given by: $A = 20(\sqrt{t}/p)$ and the stadium can accommodate no more than 10 spectators. How many talents will be hired if the maximum ticket price of 8 Euro is imposed?

5.   Restrictions on player mobility

5.1   INTRODUCTION

One regulation system that existed and, to a certain extent, still exists in the US and the European professional team sports is the so-called transfer system. In the US major leagues, it was called the reserve clause or the reservation system, abolished in the mid-seventies. In European football, it was called the (retain and) transfer system, which was abolished by the famous Bosman verdict of the European Court of Justice (1995). Without going into the details of the existing transfer systems, and the institutional differences between the US and Europe, the basic characteristic was that players were owned by a club for the length of their career. Players were not free to move to another club even at the end of their contract. A player could only change clubs if the old and new clubs reached an agreement on a transfer fee. So, players and player contracts were traded between clubs on the transfer market like, albeit well-paid, modern slaves. If a player, at the end of his contract, did not agree on the conditions of the new contract that was offered to him, or if he did not want to move to the other club, his only option was to end his career as a professional player. Some monopoly leagues tried to give this clearly illegal system a legal character by asserting that players were employed by the league, and not by the clubs. A club is only a branch of a large multi-plant company, and players are delegated by the league to the clubs. However, when they started to realise the consequences of this argument, such as also taking responsibility for the losses of the clubs, they quickly dropped the whole idea. Only the US soccer league still tries to stick to this system, which will certainly not last.

Although football players, at the end of their contract, are now free worldwide since the FIFA–EU (2001) transfer agreement, and the strict application of the transfer system is no longer in place, the player labour market is still troubled by all kinds of attempts by clubs and leagues to limit the free movement of players. One of these attempts in the FIFA–EU agreement is the compensation system for youth training or for breach of contract, which is little less than just a new name for the transfer fee. Clubs also reacted by lengthening the contract period, so that the buying and selling of contract players on the transfer market simply continued. Some players were also forced to sign a new contract with their club before the old contract expired, so that the player could be sold during his contract period. So, players may be free at the end of their contract but some can never reach that point.

The main argument to justify the introduction of a transfer system in professional team sports has always been that it is necessary for a sports league to have a reasonably balanced competition. If players are free to move to the team of their choice, they will choose the best-paying team. As a consequence, the best players all end up in the richest clubs, killing the uncertainty of outcome with the result that public interest fades. Another reason is that a transfer system helps to keep top player salaries down and increases a club's profit. In a free market, top players can sell their talents to the highest bidder. A transfer system allows club owners to capture the rents. A more positive effect of a transfer system is that player salaries will be more in line with a player's value to the league, rather then with his value to the club. This way, a transfer system provides a compensation for the inherent negative external effects that teams cause on each other by hiring players away from other teams (see Noll, 1974a).

More or less the same arguments are used to justify the so-called Rookie Draft in the US major leagues. Basically, this system comes down to a reverse-order-of-finish draft where the lowest-ranked team in the previous season is the first to select a young college player. The team with the best record is the last to pick a rookie. To prevent moral hazard, that is, low-ranked teams which intentionally lose end-of-season games in order to have the first pick, leagues have introduced a lottery system for the first round of picks. Like a transfer system, a rookie draft system also allows the financially poor teams to compete with the rich teams for new talent so that the competitive balance in a league improves (see Kahane, 2006).

In this chapter, we will analyse the impact of a transfer system on the competitive balance and player salary levels in a fixed-supply Walras equilibrium model. Again, we will consider both the profit- and the win-maximisation cases. The last section discusses the impact of the increased international mobility of players between nationally protected product markets.

5.2 THE TRANSFER SYSTEM IN A PROFIT-MAXIMISATION LEAGUE

If clubs are profit maximisers and club owners are aware of the detrimental effect of unbalanced competition, a free market for players will be self-regulating because it is in each team's own interest that it does not become too dominant. Hence restrictions to player mobility are not necessary.

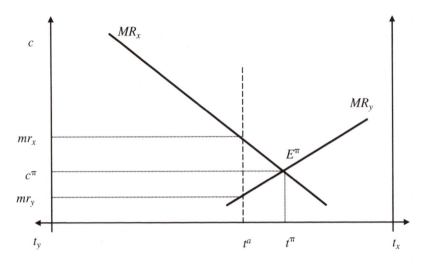

Figure 5.1   The transfer system in a profit-maximisation league

Moreover, based on the Coase theorem (1960), the so-called 'invariance proposition' states that, if clubs are profit maximisers, restrictions on the player labour market, such as a transfer system or a rookie draft, do not change the distribution of playing talent among clubs in a league compared with a competitive, free agency player market. If a player is worth more to a large-market club than to a small-market club, both clubs will easily come to an agreement to trade that player on the transfer market. The large club is willing to pay a transfer fee that is lower than the value of the player for the large club. The small club is also willing to accept a transfer fee that is higher than the value of that player for the small club. This view goes back to the seminal article on the economics of professional team sports by Rottenberg (1956). Later on, this proposition was formally proven by Quirk and El-Hodiri (1974).

Hence, with or without the transfer system, a player will end up in the team where his productivity is highest. This can be shown graphically in Figure 5.1, which reproduces the Walras competitive market equilibrium of Chapter 3. Assume that the actual distribution of talent differs from the competitive market equilibrium, say t^a. At this point, the marginal revenue of talent is much higher in the large club than in the small club: $mr_x > mr_y$. Both profit-maximising clubs can increase their profits by trading players, that is, playing talent will be sold by the small club to the large club until the difference between the marginal revenues is eliminated and thus, in Figure 5.1, t^a moves to the right until it reaches t^π. So the final outcome will be the same as the free market outcome. What is different from the free market outcome is that the small-market club receives a transfer fee for the players who are sold to the large-market club, so the small-market club's revenue is higher. This extra revenue, however, does not change the marginal revenue of talent, so the talent demand curves do not shift. The transfer money only increases the profits, or lowers the losses, of the small-market club.

In the US, where the player reservation system in the major leagues was abolished in the mid-seventies, the empirical evidence shows that there exists no correlation whatsoever between the restrictions on the player market and the competitive balance in a league. On the contrary, there is some empirical research showing an improvement in competitive balance since the introduction of free agency (see Quirk and Fort, 1992).

To a certain extent, the transfer system functioned as a kind of redistribution system: it increased the financial security of the small-market clubs that could reserve their talented players, on the one hand, or sell them for a transfer fee, on the other. Small-market clubs were clearly net sellers of talent on the transfer market. The existence of the transfer system also tempted small-market clubs to invest more in youth training because the most talented players could be sold on the transfer market.

How does a transfer market affect the player salaries in a profit-maximisation league? The player market in professional team sports under the transfer system is often cited as the classical textbook example of a monopsony. A monopsonised labour market is a market where there is just one agent on the demand side, only one employer. If players are owned by a club, or if players, due to monopoly league regulations, are not free to choose their employer, or if they are only allowed to move to another club if both clubs agree on the transfer fee, each club, or the league as a cartel of clubs, can be considered as the sole employer of professional players (see Rottenberg, 1956). Because a monopsonist is facing an upward-sloping market supply of talent, a club is no longer a wage taker on the talent market. Monopsony power allows wage setting in order to maximise profits. At the profit-maximising point, where marginal revenue equals marginal cost, the wage level, set by a monopsonist, is below marginal revenue.

This can be shown graphically. Assume that there is only one employer on the player market, which can be the league or the club. This single employer is facing the market supply of talent, which is assumed to be upward sloping. The supply curve is shown in Figure 5.2. Assume that the demand curve for talent of a profit maximiser is given by the marginal revenue curve *MR*. Talent will be hired until marginal revenue equals marginal cost. But what is the marginal cost of talent for a non-discriminating monopsonist? If a monopsonist wants to hire one more talent he has to pay a higher cost for that extra talent because the market supply curve is

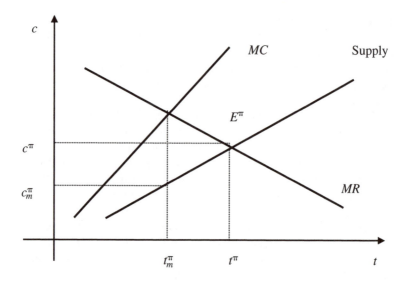

Figure 5.2   Monopsony under profit maximisation

upward sloping. But in the case of non-discrimination, that same higher salary level has to be paid to all talents that were previously hired. This will increase the marginal cost of talent by much more than just the salary of that extra playing talent. As a consequence, the marginal cost of talent (MC) can be represented in Figure 5.2 by an upward-sloping curve, above and steeper than the market supply curve. Equalising MR and MC, a profit maximiser will hire t_m^π talents, but he will only pay salary level c_m^π, because that is all he needs to pay in order to attract t_m^π talents. Comparing this outcome with the free-market outcome, where market demand equals market supply in point E^π with talent employment t^π and unit cost of talent c^π, a monopsonist hires fewer playing talents and pays lower salaries. More important is that the salary level, paid in a monopsonistic player market, is below marginal revenue. The conclusion is that, under a transfer system, players are exploited by the cartel of profit-maximising clubs.

More formally, this conclusion can be derived as follows, starting again from the club's revenue function and cost function, as specified in Chapter 3:

$$R_i = R_i[m_i, t_i] \qquad \text{and} \qquad C_i = ct_i + c_i^0.$$

If the league, as a cartel of clubs, behaves as a monopsonist in the player labour market, its season revenue (R) and cost (C) function can be written as:

$R[m,t]$ and $C = ct + c^0$

with $m = \sum_i^n m_i$ $t = \sum_i^n t_i$ $c^0 = \sum_i^n c_i^0.$

In this approach, the unit cost of a playing talent also includes the transfer fee paid minus the (expected) transfer fee received when the talent moves to another club. However, in a closed league with a fixed talent supply, the sum of all transfer fees paid by the clubs has to equal the sum of all transfer fees received by the clubs, so the unit cost of playing talent is not affected by the transfer fees. All transfer money stays within the league's money circuit.

Because the league is the sole demander of playing talent, it faces the market supply of talent, which is an upward-sloping function of the salary level:

$$c = c[t]   \text{with}   \frac{\partial c}{\partial t} > 0. \tag{5.1}$$

In a profit-maximising league, the optimality condition states that playing talent is hired until marginal revenue equals marginal cost. For a non-discriminating monopsonist, facing an upward-sloping market supply curve, the marginal labour cost will be higher than the salary level, which is no longer constant. So, the optimality condition, $MR = MC$, can be written as:

$$\frac{\partial R}{\partial t} = c + \frac{\partial c}{\partial t}t \tag{5.2}$$

From (5.1) and (5.2), it can be seen that the salary level is below marginal revenue, so the players are exploited by the owners in a profit-maximising league. It goes without saying that this monopsonistic exploitation of players under the transfer system also increases owner profits.

This theoretical result for player salary level is also supported by empirical research. Scully (1974, 1989) estimated the marginal revenue of major league baseball (MLB) players in the US in a two-step procedure. In a first step, he calculating a player's contribution to his team's winning percentage, which can be easily observed in baseball, where individual performances count more than in other team sports. In a second step, he used an econometric model to estimate the partial effect of the winning percentage on club revenue. From these figures, Scully estimated what he called the rate of monopsonistic exploitation: $RME = 1 - (c/MR)$. Scully's results were striking. Before the mid-seventies, he found a considerable degree of exploitation of the MLB players in the US. After the mid-seventies, the introduction of free agency caused a tremendous increase in player salaries, when the players managed to capture their legitimate share of the huge owner profits, and the underpayment of baseball players in the US came to an end. In a new investigation, Scully (1999) found that players were more-or-less paid according to their marginal revenue. These observations confirm what can be derived from economic theory. Moreover, Feess and Muehlheusser (2003a, 2003b) conclude from their theoretical model that the abolition of the transfer system in European football by the Bosman verdict of the European Court of Justice (1995) can have a favourable effect on investment in training, player effort and expected social welfare, and also that the new transfer agreement between FIFA and the European Commission in 2001, reintroducing compensation for youth training, has turned the clock backwards by diminishing incentives to invest in the education of young talent.

5.3   THE TRANSFER SYSTEM IN A WIN-MAXIMISATION LEAGUE

What is the impact of the transfer system on competitive balance and player salaries in a win-maximisation league? As seen before, the demand curves for talent of win-maximising clubs are given by the net average revenue (NAR) curves, presented in Figure 5.3, with E^w as the competitive market equilibrium. Starting again from a different distribution of talent t^a with unit cost of talent c^w, it is clear that the small-market club loses money, because the unit cost of talent c^w is higher than the net average revenue nar_y. The large-market club is profitable because its average revenue nar_x is higher than the unit cost of talent. If both clubs' objective is to maximise their own winning percentage under the breakeven constraint, the large-market club will try to buy more playing talents and the small-market club will want to sell talents on the transfer market. Again the distribution of talent t^a moves in the direction of the free-market distribution t^w.

There is an important difference, however, from the profit-maximisation scenario. Because the small-market club receives a transfer fee for the players it sells to the large-market clubs, its net average revenue goes up and it will use the money to increase the demand for talent. Hence, the upward shift of the small-club's average revenue curve and, consequently, the downward shift of the large-market club's average revenue curve, will result in an improved competitive balance in the league, indicated by t^{w*} (see Lavoie, 2000). The crucial question, however, is how significant this shift will be. It would be significant if the initial distribution of playing talent, that is, before clubs started to trade players on the transfer market, was more equal. But this is not the case, certainly not in Europe where there is no

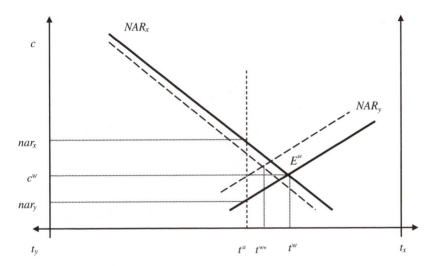

Figure 5.3   The transfer system in a win-maximisation league

rookie draft system. By definition, a small-market club is a club with a weak drawing potential, not only for spectators, but also for players, so the initial player market equilibrium under free agency is already showing an unequal distribution of talent. It follows that there is little to trade between the small- and the large-market clubs, so the distribution of talent under a transfer system will be close to the talent distribution in a competitive labour market. Only occasionally can a star player be sold by a small-market club, which will allow that club to attract one or two regular players instead. Empirical research has shown that this effect is indeed quite insignificant (see Szymanski and Kuypers, 1999). The conclusion is that, in a win-maximisation league, the transfer system can have a small positive effect on the distribution of talent among clubs and the competitive balance in a league.

One of the implications of this result is that the combination of a transfer system and a rookie draft system, in a league with win-maximising clubs, could have a more significant positive effect on the competitive balance. A reverse-order-of-finish draft can bring about a more equal distribution of talent before the trading, or the buying and selling of players starts.

In order to analyse the effect of a transfer system on player salary level, we start again from the monopsony model of the player labour market. If all clubs in a league are win maximisers, hiring as many talents as possible within the limits of their budgets, the league, as a monopsonist, can be

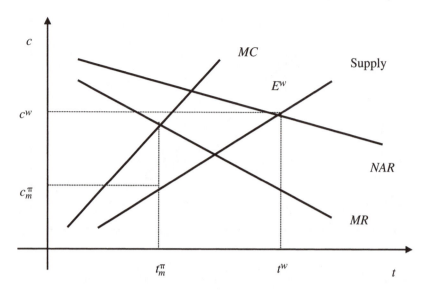

Figure 5.4   Monopsony under win maximisation

assumed to maximise the total number of talents. Playing talent will be hired until all league revenue is spent on salaries. It follows that the equilibrium point is found at the intersection of the market supply curve and the net average revenue curve (E^w), as can be seen in Figure 5.4. The salary paid by the talent-maximising and non-discriminating monopsonist has to be c^w. This salary level is clearly above marginal revenue, which means that players in a talent-maximising league, as distinct from a profit-maximising league, are not exploited by the monopsonist. On average, players are even overpaid. Moreover, the average salary level is the same as in a competitive labour market, where the equilibrium is found at the point of intersection of market demand and market supply (E^w). As a consequence, the abolition of the transfer system in a talent-maximising league does not allow any rise in average player salaries.

More formally, the objective of the talent-maximising monopsonist can be written as:

Max t   subject to: $R[m, t] - c[t]t - c^0 = 0$

where c^0 can also include a certain profit amount. The first-order conditions for talent maximisation can then be written as:

$$\frac{\partial R}{\partial t} = c + \frac{\partial c}{\partial t}t - \frac{1}{\lambda} \tag{5.3}$$

$$\frac{R - c^0}{t} = c \tag{5.4}$$

where λ is the positive Lagrange multiplier. The first equation shows that the marginal revenue is lower than the marginal cost of talent, so a talent-maximising league hires more playing talents than a profit-maximising league. The second equation indicates that the demand for talent is given by the net average revenue function. In order to show that players are no longer exploited by the monopsonist, but rather overpaid, we start from the definition of the net average revenue (*NAR*), which can be rewritten as:

$$R = \left(\frac{R - c^0}{t}\right)t + c^0, \quad \text{so} \quad MR = NAR + \frac{\partial(NAR)}{\partial t}\,t.$$

Because $\partial(NAR)/\partial t < 0$ in the relevant downward-sloping range, net average revenue is above marginal revenue. If, according to (5.4), win maximisation is reached where the net average revenue equals the unit cost of talent, the player salary level is also above marginal revenue, which means that players are on average overpaid.

Discriminating Monopsonist

Monopsonists also have the power to discriminate among players, so one cannot exclude the possibility that some players like Jean-Marc Bosman, are underpaid and exploited. A discriminating monopsonist does not pay every playing talent the same salary level. One possibility is that a discriminating monopsonist only pays the salary level he needs to pay given the market supply conditions. Facing an upward-sloping supply curve, he has to pay a higher salary to every newly hired talent, but he can discriminate because he does not have to pay that same higher salary to all previously hired talent. It follows that, in the **profit-maximisation** case, the curve of the marginal cost of talent converges on the supply curve of talent, so the profit maximising equilibrium is found in point E^π of Figure 5.2. Although this point is the same as in the competitive market equilibrium, it does not mean that there is no exploitation of players. Only the last talent hired is paid according to its marginal revenue; all other playing talents are paid below marginal revenue.

In the **win-maximisation** case, the equilibrium point of the discriminating monopsonist in Figure 5.4 is still E^w as before, but all talents are not paid the salary level c^w. Again, only the last talent hired is paid this salary; all other talents are paid less. Some players are still paid above marginal revenue, as can be seen in Figure 5.4, while others can be paid below marginal revenue.

5.4 INTERNATIONAL PLAYER MOBILITY

In most industries, one observes a very intensive international trade of goods and services and mobility of capital. Labour, however, is internationally quite immobile. Since World War II, the Europe Union has been created, with a common market, one single currency and one Central Bank. Although the European labour market has officially been deregulated as well, the international mobility of labour clearly lags behind. In the professional sports industry, however, one observes a very high degree of international player mobility while the product market is still closed and nationally protected. The Bosman verdict of the European Court of Justice (1995) abolished not only the transfer system for end-of-contract players, but also any restriction on the number of foreign European players that can be fielded. The latter ruling has caused a tremendous increase in international player mobility. The best players of the small and poor countries moved to the rich teams in the large and wealthy countries. Meanwhile, national product markets are still closed. All clubs have to play in their own national championships, which differ enormously in club and league budgets. As a consequence, the teams of small countries have to compete for the best players in an open European labour market with the teams of large countries with budgets that are more than 10 times greater. At the same time, teams in the small countries are not allowed to participate in the rich national championships of the large countries, or to compete in an open European product market.

In this section, using a simplified two-country/four-team model with quadratic club revenue functions, we analyse how the competitive balance is affected if one moves from nationally protected labour and product markets to an internationally open labour and product market. Because this model applies to Europe, rather than to the US sports markets, we assume that clubs are win maximisers. Other approaches can be found in Goossens and Késenne (2007), Haan, Koning and van Witteloostuijn (2005) and Provost (2003b).

Assume that there are two countries: A is a large country with national market size m_A and B is a small country with market size m_B, with $m = m_A + m_B$. There are two clubs in each country: club x is a large-market club and club y is a small-market club. The national markets are divided between the two clubs' local markets, so $m_A = m_{Ax} + m_{Ay}$ and $m_B = m_{Bx} + m_{By}$ with $m_A > m_B$, $m_{Ax} > m_{Ay}$ and $m_{Bx} > m_{By}$. We further assume that the following condition is fulfilled:

$$m_{Ax} - m_{Bx} < m_{ix} - m_{iy} \qquad \text{for } i = A, B. \tag{5.5}$$

This condition states that the difference between the market sizes of the two large-market clubs is smaller than the difference between the market sizes of the large- and small-market clubs in each country. This condition is clearly fulfilled in the European countries.

The season revenue of a club depends on three important factors: the size of its market, its winning percentage and the uncertainty of outcome. For each club j in country i, we specify the revenue function as follows:

$$R_{ij} = (m_{ij} + m_i/2)w_{ij} - \beta w_{ij}^2 \quad \text{for } i = A, B \quad \text{and for } j = x, y. \quad (5.6)$$

The revenue of a club depends not only on the number of stadium spectators in its local market but, increasingly so, on broadcasting and commercial revenue like sponsorship, merchandising and licensing. Because these revenue sources tend to be determined by the size of the national market, they are captured by m_i divided by the number of clubs.

The winning percentage of each team in each country is indicated by w_{ij} and is defined by:

$$w_{ij} = \frac{t_{ij}}{t_{ix} + t_{iy}} = \frac{t_{ij}}{t_i}$$

where t_{ij} is the number of playing talents of team j in country i, and t_i is the supply of talent (or the sum of talents) in country i. We assume that the supply of talent in each country can only be changed by international player mobility. The total supply of talent in both countries together is assumed to be constant and equal to t_s.

On the cost side, we consider player cost to be the sole cost of production:

$$C_{ij} = c_i t_{ij}.$$

The unit cost of talent is the same for both clubs in each country, but differs between countries.

Closed National Product and Labour Markets

The benchmark model is a closed league in each country: both the product market and the labour market are nationally protected, each club plays in its own national championship and there are no international transfers of players. In that scenario, we start from the basic assumption that the initial competitive balance between the two nations is given by their relative market size:

$$\frac{t_A}{t_B} = \frac{m_A}{m_B}.$$

(5.7)

We assume all professional football clubs in Europe to be win maximisers under the breakeven constraint, so their demand curve for talent is given by the average revenue. Even if the average revenue of each club apparently depends on the number of playing talents hired by its opponent, the non-cooperative Nash equilibrium reduces to a Walras equilibrium because the supply of talent is fixed in a closed league (see Chapter 3). Assuming that the unit cost of talent in each country is c_i, the competitive balance can be derived from $AR_{ix} = c_i = AR_{iy}$ or:

$$(m_{ix} + m_i/2) - \beta w_{ix} = (m_{iy} + m_i/2) - \beta w_{iy} \qquad \text{for } i = A, B$$

so:

$$w_{ix} - w_{iy} = \frac{m_{ix} - m_{iy}}{\beta}.$$

(5.8)

It follows that the club with the largest local market also has the best performing team.

If the closed labour market in each country is competitive, with a fixed supply of talent t_i, the equilibrium salary level in each country can also be found. The average revenue functions of the two clubs in each country can be rewritten as:

$$m_{ix} + m_i/2 - \beta w_{ix} = c_i t_i$$
$$m_{iy} + m_i/2 - \beta w_{iy} = c_i t_i$$

Summing these equations results in: $2m_i - \beta = 2c_i t_i$, so:

$$c_i = \frac{2m_i - \beta}{2t_i}.$$

(5.9)

This expression shows that the salary level is negatively related to the supply of talent, and positively to the size of the national market which affects the demand for talent. Based on ratio (5.7), one can also derive that:

$$c_A > c_B$$

which means that the salary level per unit of talent in the large country is higher than the salary level in the small country, notwithstanding the fact that a country's (innate) talents are assumed to be proportional to its market size, and that both countries show the same preference for balanced competition.

Open Labour Market and Closed Product Markets

In the second scenario, the labour market is opened so that players can move freely to the club that offers the best salaries, but the national product markets are still closed. This resembles the post-Bosman era in European football, where unlimited international transfers are possible in a common player labour market. With a given unit cost of talent c, the reaction functions are now given by:

$$AR_{ij} = c \qquad \text{for all } i \text{ and } j \tag{5.10}$$

where c is the unit cost of playing talent in the common market. Notice that in this scenario the supply of talent is flexible in each country.

A first question is how the competitive balance between the nations is affected by the deregulation of the labour market. From (5.10), one can derive that:

$$AR_{Ax} + AR_{Ay} = AR_{Bx} + AR_{By} \qquad \text{or} \qquad \frac{2m_A - \beta}{t_A} = \frac{2m_B - \beta}{t_B},$$

so the new competitive balance between the two countries becomes:

$$\frac{\widehat{t_A}}{\widehat{t_B}} = \frac{2m_A - \beta}{2m_B - \beta} > \frac{t_A}{t_B} \tag{5.11}$$

Comparing (5.11) to (5.7), it is clear that the gap between the large and small countries has widened by the deregulation of the player labour market.

A second question is how the competitive balance within each national league is affected by the liberalisation of the labour market. Because of the open player market, the supply of talent in each country has now changed to $\hat{t}_A$ and $\hat{t}_B$. Starting again from (5.10), one finds the same competitive balance in both countries as before:

$$\widehat{w_{ix}} - \widehat{w_{iy}} = \frac{m_{ix} - m_{iy}}{\beta} = w_{ix} - w_{iy}.$$

It follows that within the large and small country the competitive balance has not changed by the deregulation of the player labour market. This does not sound unreasonable because the competitive balance depends basically on the relative size of the clubs' markets. If a small country loses its best talents, a competitive labour market in that country guarantees that the 'second-best' talents are attracted by the large-market clubs in that country.

A third question is how the (international) market-clearing salary level per unit of talent is affected by deregulating the labour market. This salary level $\hat{c}$ can be derived as:

$$\hat{c} = \frac{2m_i - \beta}{2t_i'} = \frac{m - \beta}{t_s}, \qquad \text{so} \quad c_A > \hat{c} > c_B. \tag{5.12}$$

As could be expected, a comparison with the results in (5.9) shows that the market-clearing salary level per unit of talent comes down in the large country and goes up in the small country.

Open Product and Player Markets

In a third scenario, we investigate what happens if not only the labour market but also the product market are liberalised. Assume that the opening of the European product market means that the winners (the large-market teams) of each country leave the national championships and are promoted to a European division. Because these teams compete on the European product market, the variables and parameters of the revenue functions change. In revenue function (5.6) the size of the national market m_i has to be replaced by the size of the international market m, which is the sum of m_A and m_B, because these clubs can benefit from the large amounts of European broadcasting and commercial revenue. In revenue function (5.6), the winning percentage also changes, because the large-market clubs play only against each other in a European division. For these clubs, the revenue function becomes:

$$R_{ix} = (m_{ix} + m/2)\frac{t_{ix}}{t_x} - \beta\left(\frac{t_{ix}}{t_x}\right)^2 \qquad \text{for } i = A, B$$

where the total supply of talent is $t_x = t_{Ax} + t_{Bx}$. Solving the two reaction equations, one finds that the competitive balance between the two large-market clubs is:

$$\widetilde{w_{Ax}} - \widetilde{w_{Bx}} = \frac{m_{Ax} - m_{Bx}}{\beta}.$$

Comparing this result with the competitive balances in (5.8) and assuming that condition (5.5) is fulfilled, it can be derived that the competitive balance between the top clubs in the European division is more equal than the balances in the two national divisions before the opening of the product market.

The market-clearing salary level can be found to be the same as in (5.12), which indicates that the equilibrium salary level per unit of talent in the European division will be as high as the salary level before the opening of the product market.

What this chapter shows is that opening the international labour market in the professional team sports industry, with closed national product markets, creates a growing gap between the budgets and performance of the clubs in the large and small countries. Indeed, the deregulation of the European player market by the Bosman verdict of the European Court of Justice (1995) has clearly widened the gap between the football teams in the large and small countries. This analysis also shows that the balance can be restored by opening the product market of the European football industry by creating one or more European divisions, where only the best teams of each country meet, while leaving their national championships (see Hoehn and Szymanski, 1999). The existing UEFA Champions League, which is supposed to open the European football market, is actually closing it more than ever by effectively excluding 47 of the 52 European countries that the UEFA represents. With very few exceptions, only the clubs from the so-called 'Big Five' countries manage to reach the semi-finals. The only effect of the UEFA Champions League has been a devastating impact on the competitive balance both between and within countries (see Késenne, 2007b).

5.5　CONCLUSION

A general conclusion from economic theory is that, under the transfer system, players are exploited by profit-maximising club owners, but they are rather overpaid by win-maximising owners. The exploitation hypothesis under profit maximisation was well-supported by empirical research. There are also indications that the overpayment of talent under win maximisation is supported by the facts.

Regarding the competitive balance in a league, there is very little theoretical and empirical evidence that a transfer system has had any significant effect on the distribution of talent among teams.

The only advantage of the transfer system is that it enhances the financial position of the small-market clubs because they are net sellers of talent on the transfer market. It allows these clubs to survive or to increase their profits.

Economic theory also shows that an open European player and product market can close the gap between the large and small countries that has been created by only opening the European player market.

EXERCISES 5

5.1. Let the revenue function of a non-discriminating monopsonist be given by $R = 2.8t - t^2$. The cost of playing talent is the only cost, and the market supply for talent is given by $c = 0.4 + 0.5t$. What will the equilibrium demand for talent and salary level be if the monopsonist tries to maximise profits? Also calculate the RME.

5.2. With the same revenue, cost and supply functions as in exercise 5.1, calculate the equilibrium demand for talent of a discriminating profit-maximising monopsonist.

5.3. With the same revenue, cost and supply functions as in exercise 5.1, but with a win-maximising monopsonist, calculate the equilibrium demand for talent and the salary level of a non-discriminating and a discriminating monopsonist.

6.   Revenue sharing

6.1   INTRODUCTION

In most professional sports leagues, some kind of revenue sharing arrangement among clubs exists. We define revenue sharing as a distribution or redistribution of money in the sense that money that is earned by one club is given to other clubs. The main objective of revenue sharing is guaranteeing a reasonable competitive balance in a league. Given the peculiarities of the professional team sports industry, it makes sense to share club revenue. If two clubs are necessary to play a match, and more clubs to organise a championship, all participants should have a share of the success and the revenue of the championship. The fact that a championship consists of home and away games does not undermine this argument. As long as there is no free entry into the market, and relocations of teams are not allowed, the differences in market size and drawing potential of large cities versus small towns yields a lasting and unjustified advantage to the large-market teams.

The aim of this chapter is to analyse the impact of revenue sharing. Again, we will deal with both the Walras and Nash equilibrium models and distinguish between profit and win maximisation. Because the distribution of talent in a win-maximisation league is more unequal than in a profit-maximisation league, and salaries are much higher, as derived in Chapter 3, it can be argued that revenue sharing, as well as other regulations to guarantee a reasonable competitive balance and to lower top salary levels, are more needed in a win-maximisation league. We also have to distinguish between different revenue sharing arrangements because they can have a different impact. We will also consider the existing institutional differences between the American major leagues and the European professional sports leagues.

6.2   REVENUE SHARING IN THE WALRAS EQUILIBRIUM MODEL

Starting with the Walras equilibrium model, we will first consider the impact of revenue sharing in a profit-maximisation league followed by its impact in a win-maximisation league.

6.2.1   Revenue Sharing in a Profit-Maximisation League

There are several arrangements for sharing revenue. In theory, the simplest
case is where all club revenues are shared according to a single fixed share
parameter. The reality, however, is more complicated. In some leagues, the
gate receipts of every single match are shared between the home and away
team; in other leagues, only the total season broadcasting rights are shared
among all clubs. Often the broadcasting rights are monopolised and
equally redistributed by the league or based on specific criteria. Also, some
club revenues, such as local TV rights, are not shared. In most cases, a
complex combination of these arrangements exists.

One can easily derive the impact of revenue sharing by considering a
simple two-club model with club revenue functions that only depend on
market size and playing talent (see Quirk and Fort, 1992). Let R_x be the
season revenue of the large-market club and R_y the season revenue of the
small-market club. If a star indicates the after-sharing values and μ is
the share parameter, the after-sharing revenues can be written as:

$$R_x^* = \mu R_x + (1-\mu)R_y$$

with $0.5 \le \mu < 1$.

$$R_y^* = \mu R_y + (1-\mu)R_x$$

Because the demand curve for talent of a profit-maximising club is given
by the marginal revenue curve (MR), the clubs' demand curves for talent
can be written as:

$$MR_x^* = \mu MR_x - (1-\mu)MR_y$$

$$MR_y^* = \mu MR_y - (1-\mu)MR_x.$$

The switch from a positive to a negative sign by taking the first derivative
is because, given the constant supply of talent, one talent more in one team
implies one less in the other team. If market equilibrium is found where
$MR_x^* = c_\pi^* = MR_y^*$, it can easily be derived that if $MR_x^* = MR_y^*$ then $MR_x = MR_y$. It follows that revenue sharing does not change the distribution of
talent or the competitive balance in the league. It can also be shown that
revenue sharing lowers the market-clearing salary level:

$$c_\pi^* = MR_x^* = \mu MR_x - (1-\mu)MR_y = \mu c_\pi - (1-\mu)c_\pi = (2\mu-1)c_\pi.$$

Because $2\mu - 1 < 1$, the after-sharing unit cost of talent will be lower. The
reason is clear: both clubs reduce their demand for talent because they

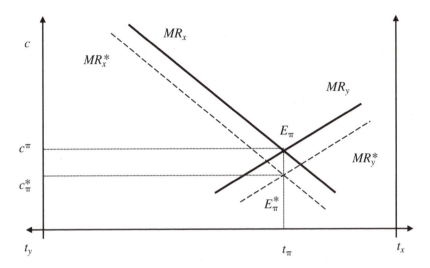

Figure 6.1   Revenue sharing under profit maximisation

have to share the revenue from hiring an extra talent with the opponent club. So, given the constant supply of talent, the equilibrium salary level comes down. In the special case of equal sharing ($\mu = 0.5$), the new market-clearing salary level will be zero. If a team has to give 50 per cent of the revenue from a newly hired talent to the other team, it is not willing to pay for talent. A possible negative effect of revenue sharing is that the investment in talent is discouraged, which reduces the absolute quality of the league.

This result is illustrated graphically in Figure 6.1, where the player market equilibrium before and after sharing is presented. The sharing arrangement reduces the marginal revenue of both clubs by the same amount at the initial equilibrium point. Because the demand functions are drawn as linear curves, it is a parallel shift. If the dotted lines are the demand curves after sharing, the new equilibrium is given by the point of intersection E_π^*. Compared with equilibrium E_π before sharing, one can see that the distribution of playing talent between both clubs is the same. The salary level, however, is lower after sharing.

It is very important to remark here that all results, based on a simplified two-club model, are not necessarily true for a more general n-club model.

In the following sections, we investigate the impact of two of the most common sharing arrangements, pool sharing and gate sharing, in a more general n-club model.

Pool sharing under profit maximisation

We start with the impact of redistributing the clubs' season revenue in a
pool sharing system with a fixed share parameter. This implies that all clubs
in a league have to contribute a fixed percentage of their season revenue to
a pool or fund, administered by the league authorities, and that the money
is redistributed equally among all clubs:

$$R_i^* = \mu R_i + \frac{(1-\mu)}{n}\sum_{j=1}^{n} R_j = \mu R_i + (1-\mu)\overline{R} \qquad \text{with} \quad 0 \le \mu < 1 \qquad (6.1)$$

where $\overline{R}$ is the average revenue in the league and μ is the share parameter. A
higher value of the share parameter means less sharing; a value of zero means
equal sharing. In order to investigate the impact of revenue sharing on the
distribution of talent, we look at the partial derivatives of the clubs' demand
curves for talent with respect to the share parameter (see Marburger, 1997a).
This methodology is based on the reasonable assumption that the competitive balance improves (worsens) if the downward shift of the demand curves
for talent of the large-market clubs is larger (smaller) than the downward
shift of the demand curves for talent of the small-market clubs. So, we need
to compare the partial derivatives of the clubs' demand curves after sharing
with respect to the share parameter at the initial market equilibrium point.

If clubs are profit maximisers, the demand curves for talent after sharing
are the marginal revenue curves after sharing:

$$\frac{\partial R_i^*}{\partial t_i} = \mu \frac{\partial R_i}{\partial t_i} + \frac{(1-\mu)}{n}\sum_{j=1}^{n} \frac{\partial R_j}{\partial t_j}\frac{\partial t_j}{\partial t_i}.$$

Given the constant supply of talent in the Walras model, one more talent
for team i implies a loss of one talent in another team, say team k, so that
$\partial t_k/\partial t_i = -1$ and:

$$\frac{\partial R_i^*}{\partial t_i} = \mu \frac{\partial R_i}{\partial t_i} + \frac{(1-\mu)}{n}\frac{\partial R_i}{\partial t_i} - \frac{(1-\mu)}{n}\frac{\partial R_k}{\partial t_k}. \qquad (6.2)$$

After taking the partial derivative of these demand curves with respect to
μ, we find that:

$$\frac{\partial(\partial R_i^*/\partial t_i)}{\partial \mu} = \frac{\partial R_i}{\partial t_i} - \frac{1}{n}\frac{\partial R_i}{\partial t_i} + \frac{1}{n}\frac{\partial R_k}{\partial t_k}.$$

Because we have to compare the shifts of the demand curves at the profit-
maximising equilibrium point where, in a competitive market, each team's

marginal revenue equals the market-clearing unit cost of talent, we can write that:

$$\frac{\partial(\partial R_i^*/\partial t_i)}{\partial \mu} = c_\pi\left(1 - \frac{1}{n} + \frac{1}{n}\right) = c_\pi. \tag{6.3}$$

Because these partial derivatives are clearly positive, revenue sharing causes a decrease in the demand for talent from all clubs. As a consequence, the unit cost of talent, or the average player salary, will also come down. The new market-clearing salary level can be derived as follows, using (6.2):

$$c_\pi^* = \frac{\partial R_i^*}{\partial t_i} = c_\pi\left(\mu + \frac{(1-\mu)}{n} - \frac{(1-\mu)}{n}\right) = \mu c_\pi.$$

A more important result from this analysis is that the distribution of talent, or the competitive balance in the league, is not affected by pool revenue sharing. As can be seen from (6.3), the shift in the demand for talent is the same in each club. All clubs equally reduce their demand for talent, because they all have to share the revenue from an extra talent with the other clubs. This result holds regardless of the specification of the revenue function and confirms Rottenberg's (1956) invariance proposition that revenue sharing does not affect the competitive balance in a profit-maximisation league.

Gate sharing under profit maximisation
Another way to share revenue, although not well-known in European professional sports, is the sharing of gate receipts. American football in the NFL (National Football League) presents the best example of this arrangement. Besides equal sharing of national broadcasting rights, the NFL home teams can only keep 60 per cent of their ticket sales; 40 per cent goes to the visiting team.

Assuming that in a championship each team plays one home and one away game against every other team, the number of games played by each team is $2(n-1)$. The revenue of club i, playing a home game against club j, is represented by R_{ij}. If the share parameter is again represented by μ, the total season revenue of each club, after sharing, can be written as:

$$R_i^* = \mu\sum_{j\neq i}^{n} R_{ij} + (1-\mu)\sum_{j\neq i}^{n} R_{ji} \qquad \text{with} \quad -0.5 \leq \mu < 1 \qquad \text{for all } i. \tag{6.4}$$

In dealing with individual games, club revenue is not only affected by the size of the market and its own winning percentage, but also by the quality of the visiting team, which can be represented by its winning percentage. Spectators prefer to watch two high-quality teams playing rather than two very poor teams, whatever the closeness of the game or the championship. Marburger (1997a), in his analysis of revenue sharing, used the number of playing talents in both teams as an approximation of the absolute quality of the play. Referring to the ticket demand function, as specified in Chapter 2, we will use the following revenue function that also includes, in a constant supply Walras equilibrium approach, the talents of the visiting team:

$$R_{ij} = R_{ij}(m_i, t_i, t_j) \qquad \text{for all } i, j \tag{6.5}$$

where the usual assumptions hold that:

$$\frac{\partial R_{ij}}{\partial m_i} > 0 \qquad \frac{\partial R_{ij}}{\partial t_j} > 0 \qquad \frac{\partial R_{ij}}{\partial t_i} > 0 \qquad \frac{\partial^2 R_{ij}}{\partial t_i^2} < 0.$$

We also assume that the impact of a team's talents on its home game attendance is larger than on the away game attendance:

$$\frac{\partial R_{ij}}{\partial t_i} > \frac{\partial R_{ji}}{\partial t_i} \qquad \text{and} \qquad \frac{\partial R_{ji}}{\partial t_j} > \frac{\partial R_{ij}}{\partial t_j}. \tag{6.6}$$

The demand curves for talent in a competitive player labour market under the profit maximisation assumption are then given by:

$$\frac{\partial R_i^*}{\partial t_i} = \mu \sum_{j \neq i}^{n} \frac{\partial R_{ij}}{\partial t_i} + (1 - \mu) \sum_{j \neq i}^{n} \frac{\partial R_{ji}}{\partial t_i} \qquad \text{for all } i.$$

Because the supply of talent is constant, a talent increase in one team implies a loss of talent in at least one other team, or, if the loss is symmetrically spread over all other teams, the change in talent of these clubs is:

$$\frac{\partial t_j}{\partial t_i} = \frac{-1}{n-1} \qquad \text{for all } i \neq j.$$

How does revenue sharing, or a decrease in the share parameter μ, affect the distribution of playing talent? We will again consider the shifts in the demand curves for talent of the large- and small-market clubs. These shifts are given by the first derivatives of the marginal revenue functions with respect to the share parameter μ:

$$\frac{\partial(\partial R_i^*/\partial t_i)}{\partial \mu} = \sum_{j \neq i}^{n} \left[\frac{\partial R_{ij}}{\partial t_i} - \frac{\partial R_{ji}}{\partial t_i} + \frac{1}{n-1} \left(\frac{\partial R_{ji}}{\partial t_j} - \frac{\partial R_{ij}}{\partial t_j} \right) \right]. \tag{6.7}$$

Based on the assumptions made in (6.6), the sign of the right-hand side of (6.7) is positive, so the demand for playing talent of each club will be reduced. As a consequence, the market-clearing player salary level will come down.

What is the impact of gate sharing on talent distribution? This can be derived again by comparing the shifts in talent demand of the large- and small-market clubs at the initial market equilibrium point. If the size of the shifts is the same for all clubs, that is, independent of i, gate sharing does not affect the distribution of talent. Unfortunately, this cannot be seen from (6.7), which is based on the general concave revenue function (6.5). A simple counter-example, however, using a quadratic revenue function, shows that revenue sharing can have a positive impact on talent distribution. Let the revenue function be specified as:

$$R_{ij} = m_i t_i - 0.5 t_i^2 + \gamma_i t_j \tag{6.8}$$

where the parameter γ_i captures the positive impact of the quality of the visiting team. We assume that its value only depends on the size of the market of club i: the larger the drawing potential of a club, the higher the value of γ_i. Given this revenue function, expression (6.7) can now be derived to be:

$$\frac{\partial(\partial R_i^*/\partial t_i)}{\partial \mu} = \frac{n(n-2)}{(n-1)}(m_i - t_i) + \frac{n}{(n-1)}[\bar{m} - \bar{t} - (n-1)\bar{\gamma}] \tag{6.9}$$

where $\bar{m}$, $\bar{t}$ and $\bar{\gamma}$ are the average values of m_i, t_i and γ_i.

In the labour market equilibrium without revenue sharing, it holds for all clubs that:

$$\frac{\partial R_i}{\partial t_i} = \sum_{i \neq j}^{n} \frac{\partial R_{ij}}{\partial t_i} = c_\pi, \quad \text{so} \quad (n-1)(m_i - t_i) - \gamma_i = c_\pi. \tag{6.10}$$

Substituting (6.10) into (6.9) yields:

$$\frac{\partial(\partial R_i^*/\partial t_i)}{\partial \mu} = \frac{n(n-2)}{(n-1)^2}(c_\pi + \gamma_i) + \frac{n}{(n-1)}[\bar{m} - \bar{t} - (n-1)\bar{\gamma}]. \tag{6.11}$$

From this result, one can see that the shifts in the demand curves for talent, caused by gate sharing, are different for every club. The higher the value of the parameter γ_i, the larger will be the downward shift in labour demand.

Because γ_i is larger for the large-market clubs, they will reduce their demand for playing talent more than the small-market clubs. It follows that the new market equilibrium after sharing shows a more equal distribution of talent, yielding a more balanced competition if clubs are profit maximisers (see Késenne, 2000a).

Remarks

1. From equation (6.11) it can be seen that gate sharing has no impact on the distribution of talent if $\gamma_i = 0$, that is, if the winning percentage, or the talents, of the visiting team do not appear in the revenue function, or if $\gamma_i = \gamma$ for all i, that is: if the impact of the visiting team's quality on revenue is the same for every club. In both cases, the downward shifts of the demand curves are the same for every club. Also, if the values of γ_i are small or the differences between the values of γ_i are small, gate sharing will be quite ineffective in changing the competitive balance in a league.
2. Expression (6.11) also indicates that, if there are only two clubs in a league ($n = 2$), gate sharing has no impact on the distribution of talent even if the parameter γ_i is different for every club. It follows that the results from a two-club model do not generally apply to a more general n-club model. Also notice that, apart from the value of the share parameter, this gate sharing arrangement and the pool sharing arrangement of the previous section are the same if there are only two clubs in the league.
3. What if a club also receives revenues that are not shared, such as local broadcasting rights in some US major leagues? From the counterexample above, it can be seen that in this case the conclusion of Fort and Quirk (1995) holds that gate sharing changes the competitive balance. If R_{ij}^0 indicates the non-shared revenues, the after-sharing revenue of each club in (6.4) has be adjusted to:

$$R_i^* = \mu \sum_{j \neq i}^{n} R_{ij} + (1 - \mu) \sum_{j \neq i}^{n} R_{ji} + \sum_{j \neq i}^{n} R_{ij}^0.$$

If the impact of t_i on the non-shared revenues is assumed to be r_i, (6.11) becomes:

$$\frac{\partial(\partial R_i^*/\partial t_i)}{\partial \mu} = \frac{n(n-2)}{(n-1)^2}(c_\pi + \gamma_i - (n-1)r_i)$$
$$+ \frac{n}{(n-1)}(\bar{m} - \bar{\imath} - (n-1)\bar{\gamma}).$$

This shows that the downward shift of the demand curve also depends on the different impact of talent on local TV rights: the larger r_i, the smaller the downward shift of the demand curve. If $\gamma_i = 0$, as Fort and Quirk (1995) assume, and r_i is larger for the large-market clubs, revenue sharing will yield a more unequal distribution of talent. If not, the outcome is theoretically indeterminate because the sign of $\gamma_i - (n-1)r_i$ is unknown.

Revenue sharing and owners' profits
An interesting question is how revenue sharing affects the profits of a club. It obviously increases the profits of the low-budget clubs, as well as total league profits. It is less clear, however, how the profits of the large-budget clubs are affected. Revenue sharing lowers the large-budget clubs' revenue, but, as has been shown above, the player labour cost is also expected to come down. In this section we will analyse the impact on profits of a pool sharing system as specified in (6.1).

Assuming that club managers are well-informed about the sharing arrangement, they will take it into account in their hiring decisions. Because revenue sharing affects talent demand and unit cost of talent, both club revenue and cost are affected. If a club's season profit is the difference between season revenue and season cost, the after-sharing profit function can be written as:

$$\pi_i^* = \mu R_i[m_i, t_i^*] + (1 - \mu)\overline{R}[m, t^*] - c^* t_i^* - c_i^0$$

where the stars indicate the after-sharing values and m and t are n vectors of the market sizes and talents. In order to analyse the impact of revenue sharing on profits, the partial derivative of the profit function with respect to μ is calculated:

$$\frac{\partial \pi_i^*}{\partial \mu} = R_i[m_i, t_i^*] - \overline{R}[m, t^*] + \frac{\partial \overline{R}[m, t^*]}{\partial \mu} + \mu\left(\frac{\partial R_i[m_i, t_i^*]}{\partial \mu} - \frac{\partial \overline{R}[m, t^*]}{\partial \mu}\right)$$

$$- c^* \frac{\partial t_i^*}{\partial \mu} - t_i^* \frac{\partial c^*}{\partial \mu} \tag{6.12}$$

A positive sign for this equation means that more revenue sharing will lower club profits.

As analysed above, revenue sharing leaves the talent distribution unchanged and lowers the competitive salary level. It follows that (6.12) simplifies to:

$$\frac{\partial \pi_i^*}{\partial \mu} = R_i[m_i, t_i] - \overline{R}[m, t] - t_i \frac{\partial c^*}{\partial \mu} = R_i[m_i, t_i] - \overline{R}[m, t] - ct_i = \pi_i - \overline{R} \quad 6.13)$$

where c is the market-clearing unit cost of talent before sharing. As has been shown before, the equilibrium unit cost of talent after sharing $c^* = \mu c$, so $\partial c^*/\partial \mu = c$. Because the right-hand side of equation (6.13) is clearly negative for all clubs that have a pre-sharing budget that is smaller than or equal to the average budget in the league, revenue sharing increases the profits of the small and mid-sized clubs. Only for teams whose pre-sharing profits are higher than the average budget in the league, will revenue sharing lower profits. Also notice that the size of the share parameter μ does not affect this result. Even the most modest sharing arrangement can lower the profits of very dominant clubs.

The positive impact of revenue sharing on league-wide profits can also be easily derived. Total league profits after sharing can be written as:

$$\sum_{i=1}^{n} \pi_i^* = \sum_{i=1}^{n} R_i[m_i, t_i^*] - \sum_{i=1}^{n} (c^* t_i^* + c_i^0).$$

Because sharing does not change the talent distribution and the supply of talent is constant, its impact on league-wide profits can be found to be:

$$\frac{\partial \sum_{i=1}^{n} \pi_i^*}{\partial \mu} = - \sum_{i=1}^{n} c t_i^* = - cs < 0.$$

Because total league revenue is not altered and the total player cost is coming down, revenue sharing increases total league profits (see Késenne, 2007).

6.2.2   Revenue Sharing in a Win-Maximisation League

In a win-maximisation league, it can be derived that revenue sharing improves the competitive balance for both the pool and the gate sharing arrangement.

Pool sharing under win maximisation
Knowing that the demand for playing talent of a win-maximising club is given by its net average revenue (NAR) curve, the clubs' demand curves after sharing are given by:

$$NAR_i^* = \frac{1}{t_i}(\mu R_i + (1 - \mu)\overline{R} - c_i^0).$$

Taking the partial derivative with respect to the share parameter yields:

$$\frac{\partial NAR_i^*}{\partial \mu} = \frac{1}{t_i}(R_i - \overline{R}) \tag{6.14}$$

Because the right-hand side of this equation is clearly positive for a large-budget club, its demand curve for playing talent shifts downwards if the degree of revenue sharing increases. For a small-budget club, the demand curve for playing talent shifts upwards. A club with a budget that is exactly equal to the average budget in the league will not change its demand for talent. If the small-market clubs are the less-talented low-budget clubs, its follows that this revenue sharing arrangement improves the distribution of playing talent in a win-maximisation league. However, if the capital costs of the large-market clubs are so high that they become the less-talented clubs in the league, revenue sharing can worsen the competitive balance.

Revenue sharing can also increase the salary level. This can be derived as follows. If the distribution of talent in a win-maximisation league is more unequal than in a profit-maximisation league, and revenue sharing improves the competitive balance, it moves the distribution of talent closer to the profit maximising distribution of talent, where total league revenue is at its maximum level (see Chapter 3). Because the equilibrium salary level in the win maximisation equilibrium is equal to the league's net revenue divided by the constant and normalised supply of playing talent, that is, $c_w = 2/n\Sigma_{j=1}^{n}(R_j - c_j^0)$, the salary reaches its highest level when total league revenue is at its highest level. It follows that revenue sharing can increase the salary level in a win maximising league.

In Figure 6.2 this can be shown graphically for a two-club model. After revenue sharing, the larger-market club's demand curve for talent has shifted downwards whereas the small-market club's demand curve has shifted upwards, so the new market equilibrium results in a more balanced distribution of playing talent. Because the upward shift of the demand curve of the large-budget club is smaller then the downward shift of the demand curve of small-budget club, the after-sharing salary will be higher.

Gate sharing under win maximisation
If the demand for talent under win maximisation is given by the net average revenue curve, and if gate revenues are shared according to a sharing arrangement (6.4), the demand for talent after sharing can be written as:

$$NAR_i^* = \frac{1}{t_i}\left(\mu \sum_{j \neq i}^{n} R_{ij} + (1 - \mu) \sum_{j \neq i}^{n} R_{ji} \right) - \frac{c_i^0}{t_i}.$$

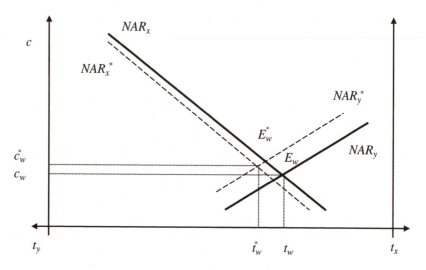

Figure 6.2   Revenue sharing under win maximisation

Taking the first-order derivative with respect to μ yields:

$$\frac{\partial NAR_i^*}{\partial \mu} = \frac{1}{t_i}\left(\sum_{j \neq i}^{n} R_{ij} - \sum_{j \neq i}^{n} R_{ji}\right). \tag{6.15}$$

The sign of this derivative indicates again the direction of the shift in the demand curves for talent. For large-budget clubs, (6.15) is positive, because $R_{ij} > R_{ji}$. For low-budget clubs, (6.15) is negative. It follows that large-budget clubs will lower their talent demand and low-budget clubs will increase their demand for talent. The result is a more equal distribution of playing talent and a more balanced league championship. If large-market clubs are interested in a higher profit rate, they will spend less money on playing talent and contribute to a more equal distribution of playing talent this way.

The impact of gate sharing on the salary level in a win-maximisation league is the same as the impact of pool sharing.

Remarks

1. It is possible that in the win-maximisation equilibrium, at the point of intersection of the average revenue curves, the marginal revenue of the large-market club may be negative. Its winning percentage can be so high that, because of a lack of uncertainty of outcome, public interest

fades and total season revenue decreases. In that case, revenue sharing can increase not only the season revenue of the small-market club, but also the season revenue of the large-market club if the increase in revenue, due to a more tense competition, outbalances the negative effect on its revenue (see Késenne, 1996).

2. It is also worth considering the Rascher (1997) utility-maximisation model, which assumes that clubs are maximising a linear combination of profit and wins (or talent), given by the following function:

$$u_i = \pi_i + \alpha_i t_i = (R_i - ct_i - c_i^0) + \alpha_i t_i \qquad \text{with} \quad a_i > 0.$$

If $a_i > 1$ more weight is put on wins. The impact of the share parameter μ on the demand for playing talent in this model is the same as the right-hand side of (6.7). This indicates again that revenue sharing causes a reduction in the demand for talent by all clubs and a decrease in the salary level. However, contrary to the profit-maximisation model, the reduction of playing talent is not the same in every club. If clubs have different levels of motivation for winning, revenue sharing changes the distribution of playing talent. This can be shown again by the counter-example. Given revenue function (6.8), expression (6.11) becomes:

$$\frac{n(n-2)}{(n-1)^2}(c_{\pi w} + \gamma_i - \alpha_i) + \frac{n}{(n-1)}[\overline{m} - \overline{\iota} - (n-1)\overline{\gamma}].$$

First of all, if there are only two clubs in the league, revenue sharing has no impact on the distribution of playing talent. But if $n > 2$ the first term indicates that the reaction of each club to revenue sharing also depends on its level of motivation for winning α_i. It turns out that a club that shows a greater interest in profit making will reduce its demand for playing talent more than a club with a strong motivation for winning. The conclusion is that, under the reasonable assumption that large-market clubs care more about profits, revenue sharing causes a stronger downward shift in their demand for talent, so revenue sharing has a positive impact on the distribution of playing talent. The same result can be found for a pool sharing system.

3. In the quadratic revenue functions above, clubs only differ in market size, so the large-market clubs dominate the small-market clubs in terms of talent. However, if the slopes of the demand curves, given by the parameter β_i in the quadratic revenue function $R_i = m_i t_i - \beta_i t_i^2$, are also different, it is possible that the small-market club dominates the large-market club (see Remark 1 in Section 3.3, p. 42). In this rather

exceptional case, revenue sharing can have a possibly unwanted effect on the distribution of talent in a win-maximisation league. The revenue sharing arrangements above still improve the competitive balance, but in this case, the ill-performing large-market club profits from the sharing arrangement to the disadvantage of the well-performing small-market club. The reason is that the small-market club also has the largest budget if it is more talented than the large-market club. Moreover, in this situation, revenue sharing implies a loss of total league revenue, because the distribution of talent is moving away from the efficient allocation of talent which is reached in the profit-maximisation equilibrium. Therefore, one might consider a sharing system that is not based on the size of the budget, but on the size of the market. The following sharing arrangement can serve as an example:

$$R_i^* = R_i - \frac{1}{\mu}(m_i - \overline{m}) \qquad \text{with} \quad \mu > 0$$

where $\overline{m}$ is the average market size in the league. Again a higher value of the parameter μ means less sharing. This sharing arrangement implies a money transfer from the large-market to the small-market club and not from the high-budget to the low-budget club. This arrangement not only has the advantage of establishing a more balanced competition, but also avoids the disadvantage that the small-market club is punished for performing better than the large-market club. Moreover, this sharing arrangement increases total league revenue because it moves the win-maximisation equilibrium closer to the profit-maximisation equilibrium.

In a profit-maximisation league, this sharing arrangement does not change the competitive balance because the marginal revenue is not affected.

6.3 REVENUE SHARING IN THE NASH EQUILIBRIUM MODEL

Most studies dealing with the impact of revenue sharing start from the assumption that the supply of talent is fixed (see Fort and Quirk, 1995). Moreover, they also assume that team owners take this fixed talent supply into account in their hiring decisions. Team owners know that one extra talent not only strengthens their own team, but that it also weakens another team in the league. Hence owners can internalise the negative externality that talent hiring causes on the other teams. In this approach, one club's demand for talent is not affected by the hiring strategies of other clubs;

owners can choose the winning percentage of their team. If the externalities are not internalised, or if the supply of talent is flexible, we have seen in Chapter 3 that the equilibrium distribution of talent and salary level can be different. In this section we will concentrate on the Nash equilibrium in the flexible-supply case. The game that is considered is again a non-cooperative game, where all teams decide on the hiring of talents, taking into account the talent hiring of their opponents in the league. We start with the case of an exogenously given marginal cost of talent. The last two sections consider the case of non-proportional sharing, based on a prize fund, and the case of an efficiency wage.

6.3.1 Exogenous Salary Level

As distinct from the result in the Walras equilibrium model, it can be shown that in a two-club Nash equilibrium model, revenue sharing worsens the competitive balance under the **profit-maximisation** hypothesis (see Szymanski and Késenne, 2004). This can be explained by the fact that revenue sharing partly neutralises the negative external effects that clubs have on each other when hiring talent, because revenue sharing lowers the marginal revenue from talent. Given that the large-market club has a higher marginal revenue from talent, the negative external effect that the small-market club has on the large-market club is larger than the external effect that the large-market club has on the small-market club, so the small-market club is worse off if these externalities are partly neutralised.

This can be shown using a simple model. Assume that the revenue function of the large-market team is $R_x = \alpha w_x$ with $\alpha > 1$ and the revenue function of the small-market club is $R_y = w_y$. Because $w_x = t_x/(t_x + t_y)$ and $w_y = t_y/(t_x + t_y)$ these revenue functions are concave in talent. With a constant marginal cost of talent, the Nash equilibrium can then be found at the point of intersection of the reaction curves:

$$\frac{\alpha t_y}{(t_x + t_y)^2} = \frac{t_x}{(t_x + t_y)^2}$$

so the solution is $t_x/t_y = \alpha > 1$. The large-market club is more talented than the small-market club. If revenues are shared, with a star indicating the after-sharing values, revenues are:

$$R_x^* = \mu \alpha w_x + (1 - \mu) w_y$$
$$R_y^* = \mu w_y + (1 - \mu) \alpha w_x.$$

The new Nash equilibrium is then found where:

$$\frac{\partial R_x^*}{\partial t_x} = \frac{\mu\alpha t_y - (1-\mu)t_y}{(t_x+t_y)^2} = \frac{\partial R_y^*}{\partial t_y} = \frac{\mu t_x - (1-\mu)\alpha t_x}{(t_x+t_y)^2}.$$

The solution

$$\frac{t_x^*}{t_y^*} = \frac{\mu\alpha + \mu - 1}{\mu\alpha + \mu - \alpha} > \alpha$$

indicates that revenue sharing worsens the competitive balance (see Szymanski, 2003).

Another implication of revenue sharing in a model with a flexible talent supply is that, with a given salary level, the number of talents hired by each club decreases. This can be seen by comparing the demand for talent before and after sharing. Because $\mu\alpha - (1-\mu) < \alpha$ and $\mu - (1-\mu)\alpha < 1$, it follows that the league is less talented, so the absolute quality of play diminishes, which can have a negative effect on attendances, gate receipts and other club revenues (see also Provost, 2003a).

It can be shown that these results also hold for an n-club model with more general revenue functions (see Késenne, 2005). To show this, let us start from the pool sharing system in (6.1), which is repeated here:

$$R_i^* = \mu R_i + \frac{(1-\mu)}{n}\sum_{j=1}^n R_j = \mu R_i + (1-\mu)\overline{R}.$$

To find the impact of this sharing system on the distribution of talent, we will investigate again the shifts of the teams' demand curves for talent. The assumption is that revenue sharing worsens the competitive balance if, for any pair of clubs in the league, the downward shift of the demand curve of the high-talented club is smaller than the downward shift of the demand curve of the low-talented club at the initial player market equilibrium point.

If a club is a profit maximiser, its demand curve for talent is given by the marginal revenue:

$$\frac{\partial R_i^*}{\partial t_i} = \mu\frac{\partial R_i}{\partial t_i} + \frac{(1-\mu)}{n}\frac{\partial R_i}{\partial t_i} + \frac{(1-\mu)}{n}\sum_{j\neq i}^n\frac{\partial R_j}{\partial t_i}.$$

The size of the shifts of these demand curves are given by the partial derivative of this marginal revenue function with respect to the share parameter μ:

$$\frac{\partial(\partial R_i^*/\partial t_i)}{\partial \mu} = \frac{(n-1)}{n}\frac{\partial R_i}{\partial t_i} - \frac{1}{n}\sum_{j \neq i}^{n}\frac{\partial R_j}{\partial t_i} \qquad (6.16)$$

Because this expression is clearly positive, revenue sharing causes all clubs to reduce their demand for playing talent. More important is the size of these shifts at the initial equilibrium point, that is, at the point where the club's marginal revenue equals the market-clearing unit cost of talent before sharing:

$$\frac{\partial R_i}{\partial t_i} = \frac{\partial R_i}{\partial w_i}\frac{\partial w_i}{\partial t_i} = c_\pi \qquad \text{for all } i. \qquad (6.17)$$

By substituting (6.17) into (6.16) for all clubs, and given that $\partial R_j/\partial t_i$ can also be written as:

$$\frac{\dfrac{\partial R_j}{\partial w_j}\dfrac{\partial w_j}{\partial t_i}\dfrac{\partial w_j}{\partial t_j}}{\dfrac{\partial w_j}{\partial t_j}}$$

one finds that:

$$\frac{\partial(\partial R_i^*/\partial t_i)}{\partial \mu} = \frac{(n-1)}{n}c_\pi - \frac{1}{n}\sum_{j \neq i}^{n}c_\pi\frac{\partial w_j}{\partial t_i} \Big/ \frac{\partial w_j}{\partial t_j} = c_\pi\left\{\frac{(n-1)}{n} + \frac{1}{n}\sum_{j \neq i}^{n}\left(\frac{t_j}{\sum_{k \neq j}^{n}t_k}\right)\right\}$$

$$(6.18)$$

From this result it can be derived that club i with a high number of playing talents before sharing (which is in this general model not necessarily the large-market club), will reduce its demand for talent less than club k with a low number of playing talents:

$$\text{if} \quad t_i > t_k \qquad \text{then} \qquad \frac{\partial(\partial R_i^*/\partial t_i)}{\partial \mu} < \frac{\partial(\partial R_k^*/\partial t_k)}{\partial \mu}. \qquad (6.19)$$

It follows that this revenue sharing arrangement worsens the competitive balance.

A numerical example with only three clubs in the league can illustrate this result. For the three clubs, the downward shifts of the demand curves, according to expression (6.18), are:

club 1: $c\left\{\dfrac{2}{3}+\dfrac{1}{3}\left(\dfrac{t_2}{t_1+t_3}+\dfrac{t_3}{t_1+t_2}\right)\right\}$

club 2: $c\left\{\dfrac{2}{3}+\dfrac{1}{3}\left(\dfrac{t_1}{t_2+t_3}+\dfrac{t_3}{t_1+t_2}\right)\right\}$

club 3: $c\left\{\dfrac{2}{3}+\dfrac{1}{3}\left(\dfrac{t_1}{t_2+t_3}+\dfrac{t_2}{t_1+t_3}\right)\right\}.$

Comparing these shifts, it is clear that, if $t_1 > t_2 > t_3$, the shift of the demand curve of club 1 is smaller than the shift of club 2, which is again smaller than the shift of club 3, which confirms the general result in (6.19).

Remarks

1. Expression (6.18) also shows that, if the number of teams in the league is very high, the term between brackets approaches one, so the downward shift in demand for talent from all teams is more-or-less the same. It follows that in this case the invariance proposition still holds that revenue sharing does not affect the competitive balance. This result also confirms a well-known general proposition that a non-cooperative Nash equilibrium approaches a Walras equilibrium if the number of firms increases.

2. It is worthwhile considering again the player market equilibrium in the fixed-supply Nash and Walras equilibria as presented by Figure 3.8, which is repeated here in Figure 6.3. Assume that we are in the Nash equilibrium, at the point of intersection of the dotted non-linear demand curves, and the league introduces an equal, 50/50, sharing system. Revenue sharing will not only worsen the competitive balance; the distribution of talent will be the same as the market equilibrium in the Walras equilibrium model, with a salary level equal to zero. The reason is that, by a 50/50 sharing system, the negative externalities are fully neutralised as they are in a Walras model where the externalities are assumed to be internalised. No team is willing to pay for playing talent; it is the league that hires, allocates and pays the players. The allocation of playing talents is optimal, and total league revenue and profits are maximised (joint profit maximisation). As shown in Figure 6.3, the 50/50 sharing arrangement causes a downward shift of both non-linear demand curves such that the new point of intersection is found at the horizontal axis, where the distribution of talent is the same as at the point of intersection of the linear demand curves, and the unit cost of talent is zero.

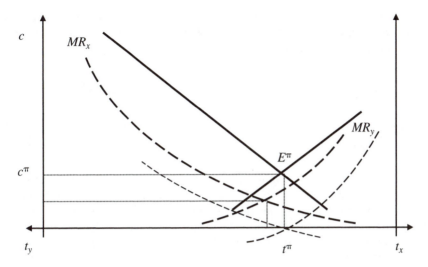

Figure 6.3   Fixed-supply Walras and Nash equilibria

3. Whereas the pool sharing system arrangement worsens the competitive balance if all clubs are profit maximisers, it is obvious that revenue sharing improves the competitive balance if clubs are win maximisers, even if the talent supply is flexible. As shown in Chapter 3, the flexible-supply Nash equilibrium and the fixed-supply Walras equilibrium are identical. Because the demand curves for talent are given by the net average revenue curves, the impact of pool sharing is the same as given by solution (6.14). Because sharing increases the total revenue of those clubs that have a lower revenue than the average revenue in the league, and win-maximising clubs spend all their (net) revenue on talent, the result is an improved competitive balance (see also Provost, 2003a).

4. It is also possible that in one league, some clubs are profit maximisers and others are win maximisers. In the most likely case of the poorer clubs being win maximisers and the richer clubs being profit maximisers, the impact of revenue sharing is clear. Because the poor clubs will increase their demand for talent and the rich clubs will reduce theirs, the impact of revenue sharing is a better competitive balance.

Impact of revenue sharing on owner profits
If the impact of revenue sharing on the distribution of playing talents is different in the Nash equilibrium model compared with the Walras equilibrium model, the impact of revenue sharing on profits can also be

expected to be different. This can be analysed starting again from equation
(6.12), where the partial derivative of the after-sharing profit function with
respect to μ is given and which is repeated here:

$$\frac{\partial \pi_i^*}{\partial \mu} = R_i[m_i, t_i^*] - \overline{R}[m, t^*] + \frac{\partial \overline{R}[m, t^*]}{\partial \mu} + \mu\left(\frac{\partial R_i[m_i, t_i^*]}{\partial \mu} - \frac{\partial \overline{R}[m, t^*]}{\partial \mu}\right)$$

$$- c^* \frac{\partial t_i^*}{\partial \mu} - t_i^* \frac{\partial c^*}{\partial \mu} \tag{6.20}$$

Remember that a higher value of μ means less sharing and that a positive
sign of this equation means that more revenue sharing will lower club
profits. Whereas it is obvious that revenue sharing increases the profits of
the small-market clubs, the outcome for the large-market clubs is theoretically undetermined in both the flexible- and the fixed-supply model (see
Késenne, 2007a).

In this section we will only investigate the impact of revenue sharing on
the profits of a medium-sized club with an average market size $\overline{m}_i$. For a
medium-sized club, the sum of the first five terms in equation (6.20) is zero
in both the flexible-supply and the fixed-supply models. In the flexible-
supply model with an exogenous salary level, that is, $\partial c^*/\partial \mu = 0$, it has been
shown above that all clubs reduce their demand for talent, resulting in a
more unbalanced competition if revenues are shared. It follows that for a
medium-sized club $\partial t_i^*/\partial \mu > 0$. In the fixed-supply model, revenue sharing
also worsens the competitive balance but without changing the demand
from a medium-sized club. The equilibrium salary level will now decrease.
This implies that for a medium sized club $\partial t_i^*/\partial \mu = 0$ and $\partial c^*/\partial \mu > 0$. It
follows that it holds in both cases that:

$$\frac{\partial \pi_i^*}{\partial \mu} = - c^* \frac{\partial t_i^*}{\partial \mu} - t_i^* \frac{\partial c^*}{\partial \mu} < 0 \tag{6.21}$$

Revenue sharing only lowers the club's cost without changing its revenue,
so the profits of a medium-sized club go up. Only if a decrease in total
talent supply reduces the absolute equality of the league, or a worse competitive balance reduces public interest, might a negative effect on club
revenue occur, but this is unlikely to offset the cost effect.

6.3.2   Prize Funds

So far, we have assumed that the contribution of each club to the pool is
linked to the size of its budget and that the money is redistributed equally,

and not linked to the TV coverage or to any performance variable such as the winning percentage, or the quality of youth training. Using a simplified model, Szymanski (2003) has investigated the impact of a sharing system where each team has to contribute a fixed amount to a prize fund that is redistributed according to the winning percentage of the team. The two-club model is the same as in section 6.3.1. If the revenue function of the large-market team is $R_x = \alpha w_x$ with $\alpha > 1$ and that of the small-market club is $R_y = w_y$, we have seen that the Nash equilibrium yields the solution for the competitive balance: $t_x / t_y = \alpha$. Assume that a fund v is created with an equal contribution $v/2$ by each club. Each club receives a share of that fund according to its winning percentage, that is, $w_x v$ and $w_y v$. If a star indicates again the after-sharing values, we find that:

$$R_x^* = \alpha w_x - v/2 + w_x v$$

$$R_y^* = w_y - v/2 + w_y v.$$

The Nash equilibrium can then be found at the point of intersection of the reaction functions $(\alpha + v)t_y / (t_x + t_y)^2 = (1 + v)t_x / (t_x + t_y)^2$ so that the new competitive balance is $t_x^* / t_y^* = (\alpha + v)/(1 + v) < \alpha$. What the simple model shows is that this specific revenue sharing system improves the competitive balance. This can again be explained by referring to the external effects that clubs have on each other when hiring talent. In this sharing arrangement, the contribution of each club is no longer linked to its marginal revenue of talent, so the externalities are not neutralised. Moreover, by rewarding winning, both the small- and large-market clubs gain from winning, which enforces the larger negative external effects that small-market clubs have on large-market clubs.

6.3.3 Efficiency Wages

The owner may determine the salary level by taking into account that the salary level influences the effort players are willing to make. In this case, how does revenue sharing affect the salary level? By offering higher salaries, a team owner can also try to attract the best players or to stop the best players from leaving the team. Referring to section 3.4.5, where the efficiency wage theory was introduced in the Nash equilibrium model, the central question in this section is how revenue sharing affects the efficiency wage set by the owners.

Starting again from the simple pool sharing system in (6.1), and assuming for simplicity that the efficiency salary level of one team does not affect the effort of the players in another team, the marginal revenues with respect to salary and talent after sharing are:

$$\frac{\partial R_i^*}{\partial c_i} = \left(\frac{n\mu + 1 - \mu}{n}\right)\frac{\partial R_i}{\partial c_i} = t_i$$

$$\frac{\partial R_i^*}{\partial t_i} = \left(\frac{n\mu + 1 - \mu}{n}\right)\frac{\partial R_i}{\partial t_i} + \frac{1 - \mu}{n}\sum_{j \neq i}^{n}\frac{\partial R_j}{\partial t_i} = c_i.$$

After substituting the expressions (3.21) and (3.22) into these equations, one can find the after-sharing effort elasticity in a profit-maximisation league as:

$$\varepsilon_i^{\pi*} = \left(\frac{c_i}{c_i - \frac{1 - \mu}{n}\sum_{j \neq i}^{n}\frac{\partial R_j}{\partial t_i}}\right)\frac{\sum_{j \neq i}^{n} t_j}{\sum_j^n t_j} < \varepsilon_i^{\pi}.$$

In a win-maximisation league, referring again to the results of Chapter 3, the after-sharing effort elasticity is:

$$\varepsilon_i^{w*} = \left(\frac{c_i}{c_i - 1/\lambda_i - \frac{1 - \mu}{n}\sum_{j \neq i}^{n}\frac{\partial R_j}{\partial t_i}}\right)\frac{\sum_{j \neq i}^{n} t_j}{\sum_j^n t_j} < \varepsilon_i^{w}.$$

Because $\sum_{j \neq i}^{n} \partial R_j / \partial t_i$ is negative, this lower effort elasticity suggests that a higher efficiency wage level is set by the owners in both a profit- and a win-maximization league, due to the revenue sharing arrangement. Also, the more revenue is shared (that is, the lower μ), the higher the efficiency wage will be. This result is quite different from the result in all other models, where revenue sharing lowers the player salary level.

How revenue sharing changes the competitive balance in a profit- or win-maximisation league is an open question. It will depend on the size of the efficiency wage changes of large- and small-market clubs that are caused by the sharing arrangement. However, it can be expected that revenue sharing will still improve the competitive balance in a win-maximisation league when efficiency wages are set by the owners, because the difference between the wage changes in large- and small-market clubs has to be extremely large in order to offset the difference in club revenue caused by the sharing arrangement (see Késenne 2006).

6.4 CONCLUSION

The case for revenue sharing in a **profit-maximisation** league is not very strong. In the benchmark scenario of Rothenberg (1956) and Quirk and El Hodiri (1974), revenue sharing does not affect the competitive balance. Moreover, the distribution of talent is optimal in terms of total league revenue if clubs are profit maximisers, so revenue sharing, which leads to a less efficient allocation of talent, is not needed. So far, to the best of our knowledge, the impact of revenue sharing in the most realistic scenario has not been analysed. This scenario should include a league with more than two clubs, where club revenue is affected by both the winning percentage of the home and the visiting teams, where the revenue sharing system is based on the sharing of gate receipts, the pool sharing of broadcasting rights and the non-sharing of other revenue, and where the talent supply can be fixed or flexible, but analysed using the appropriate model. Some partial results, taking into account deviations from the initial benchmark scenario, show that revenue sharing can improve or worsen the competitive balance, which leads to the general conclusion that the impact of revenue sharing on competitive balance can be expected to be quite limited in the profit-maximisation scenario.

In the North American major leagues, clubs are assumed to be profit maximisers; the supply of talent is constant and assumed to be internalised by the hiring strategy of the owners; some club revenues are shared, like gate receipts in NFL (National Football League) and MLB (Major League Baseball); and the national broadcasting rights are pooled and redistributed, but local television rights are not shared. In such a case, revenue sharing cannot be expected to have a strong effect on competitive balance.

If all clubs are **win maximisers**, the theory shows that revenue sharing is effective in establishing a more balanced distribution of talent among large- and small-market clubs. Moreover, it can be expected that, without any sharing, the distribution of talent in a win-maximisation league is more unequal than in a profit-maximisation league. Also, the distribution of talent without sharing is suboptimal in terms of total league revenue, because of the inefficient allocation of talent among clubs. In the national soccer leagues in Europe, where clubs are assumed to behave like win or utility maximisers, revenue sharing will be even more appropriate after the abolition of the transfer system by the Bosman verdict. The small-market clubs, being net sellers of talent on the transfer market, complain about a dramatic loss of revenue. If the transfer market has partially functioned as a redistribution system between large- and small-market clubs, revenue sharing might remedy the weak financial position of the small-market clubs.

EXERCISES 6

6.1. If in a two-club league with revenue functions:

$$R_x = 160t_x - 100t_x^2 \quad \text{and} \quad R_y = 120t_y - 100t_y^2,$$

the share parameter in the gate sharing arrangement is $\mu = 0.8$, derive the distribution of talent and the equilibrium salary level if both clubs are profit maximisers (before sharing, $t_x^\pi = 0.6$, $t_y^\pi = 0.4$ and $c^\pi = 40$).

6.2. Assuming the following club revenue functions:

$$R_x = 200t_x - 100t_x^2 \quad \text{and} \quad R_y = 80t_y - 100t_y^2$$

and only player costs, derive the average club revenue, the clubs' profits and total league profits for the following share parameter values in a pool sharing system: $\mu = 1, 0.5$ and 0. What do you conclude concerning the impact of revenue sharing on profits?

6.3. Let the revenue functions of the large- and the small-market club again be given by:

$$R_x = 160t_x - 100t_x^2 \quad \text{and} \quad R_y = 120t_y - 100t_y^2.$$

In Chapter 3, we found that the distribution of talent was $t_x^w/t_y^w = 0.7/0.3$ under win maximisation and $t_x^\pi/t_y^\pi = 0.6/0.4$ under profit maximisation. Assume now that the following sharing arrangement is imposed:

$$R_i^* = R_i - \frac{t_i}{\mu}(m_i - \overline{m}) \quad \text{with} \quad \mu = 2.$$

How does this sharing system affect the distribution of talent in a win- and a profit-maximisation league?

6.4. Starting from the quadratic revenue functions in a two-club model:

$$R_x = m_x w_x - b w_x^2$$

$$\text{with} \quad w_x = \frac{t_x}{t_x + t_y} \quad \text{and} \quad w_y = \frac{t_y}{t_x + t_y}$$

$$R_y = m_y w_y - b w_{y_s}^2$$

and with a fixed supply of talent equal to one, derive the distribution of talent if a 50/50 sharing arrangement is imposed in a profit-maximisation league.

7. Salary caps

7.1 INTRODUCTION

After the abolition of the reservation system and the end of the mono-psonistic exploitation of players in the North American major leagues in the mid-seventies, player salaries went up dramatically, and consequently, club owner profits took a nosedive. In reaction to this profit squeeze, league administrators and club owners looked for an alternative regulation system to guarantee a reasonable profit rate. One of these alternatives is generally known as a salary cap. In Europe, the introduction of salary caps has also been discussed recently, but primarily to keep clubs from running into heavy financial losses. In fact, a salary cap is a misleading term. In most cases, it is not a cap on the individual player's salary level, but a ceiling to a club's season payroll, which is the total amount that a club can pay on player salaries. Nevertheless, different types of salary caps can be distinguished. There are hard salary caps and soft caps, that is, luxury taxes. The cap can be the same fixed amount for every club in the league, or it can be a percentage of a club's total budget; it can also be at the same time a floor, so cross-subsidisation is sometimes needed. Also, individual salary caps exist. In this chapter, we will investigate how different types of salary caps affect the distribution of talent, the salary level, owner profits and the ticket price in an internalised fixed-supply model.

7.2 NORTH AMERICAN PAYROLL CAP

In a review article on cross-subsidisation in team sports, Fort and Quirk (1995) conclude that a salary cap is the only cross-subsidisation scheme currently in use that can be expected to accomplish both the financial viability of small-market teams and a better competitive balance in a league. The salary cap these authors are dealing with is the typical payroll cap that is imposed in North American major leagues such as the NBA. It is a maximum amount that clubs are allowed to spend on player salaries in one season. The cap is calculated as a percentage of defined gross revenue of the league, based on the total revenue of all the clubs together during the previous season, divided by the number of clubs in the league:

$$cap = \frac{\alpha \sum_{i=1}^{n} R^*_{i,-1}}{n} \qquad \alpha < 1. \tag{7.1}$$

It follows that the amount of the cap is the same for all clubs. Both the gross revenue of the league $R^*_{i,-1}$ and the percentage α are determined in a collective bargaining agreement between the club owners and the players association. In fact, an NBA style of salary cap is not only a cap on the total payroll of a team, it is also a floor. The low-budget clubs are forced to pay the same amount on player salaries, so some cross-subsidisation among clubs is required to accommodate the possible financial losses that the cap might create. It follows that this regulation system is rather a combination of a salary cap and a revenue sharing arrangement. In theory, the clubs' equal spending on talent also creates an equal distribution of talent and a lower salary level (see Quirk and Fort, 1992).

In this section we will analyse the impact of this payroll cap, with and without the floor, on the competitive balance in the league, on the average player salary level, on the owner profits and on total league revenue. We will again consider the profit-maximisation and win-maximisation cases.

7.2.1 Profit Maximisation

In a competitive player labour market of a profit maximisation league, imposing the payroll cap (7.1) means that:

$$ct_i \le cap, \qquad \text{so} \qquad c \le \frac{cap}{t_i} \qquad \text{for all } i.$$

This implies that the cap line is a simple hyperbolic function; this can easily be represented graphically for a two-club model in Figure 7.1, where x is again the large-market club and y the small-market club. We assume that the salary cap is not effective for the small-market club because it cannot afford to pay the amount of the cap.

If the payroll cap is not a floor, the cap does not affect the demand for talent by the low-budget club. As can be seen, the low-budget club's demand curve is below the cap line. The high-budget club's demand curve is above the cap line; its payroll ct_x, which can be represented by a rectangle in this diagram, has to stay below the hyperbolic function cap_x. The high-budget club will try to get as close a possible to its profit-maximising demand curve, so the hyperbole becomes its new demand curve for talent. The new market

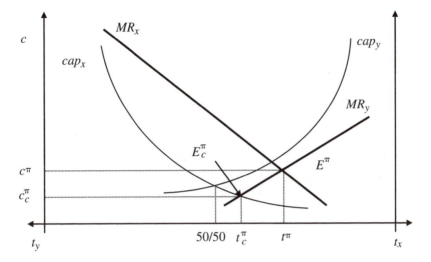

Figure 7.1   Payroll cap

equilibrium is now found at E_c^π, the point of intersection of the marginal revenue of the low-budget club MR_y and the hyperbolic cap_x so:

$$MR_y = \frac{cap}{t_x}.$$

The result is a more equal distribution of talent t_c^π and a lower salary level c_c^π.

The impact of the salary cap on owner profits can also be derived from this diagram. A club's profits can be represented by the area below the demand curve and above the salary level. In Figure 7.2, one can see that the move from equilibrium point E^π to E_c^π implies a clear increase in the profits of the low-budget club. The profits of the high-budget club also increase because the increase in profits, caused by the lower salary level (the shaded rectangle in Figure 7.2), more than compensates for the decrease in profits, caused by the lower talent demand (the shaded triangle).

If player salaries go down and owner profits go up, what happens to total league revenue? The loss in player salaries turns out to be larger than the gain in owner profits because the new equilibrium deviates from the free-market profit-maximising equilibrium. It follows that total league revenue comes down by imposing the salary cap, the loss being as large as the triangle $E^\pi E_c^\pi E_c$. The reason is again that the allocation of playing talent is not efficient: some talents are not playing for the team where their marginal product is at its maximum level (see Késenne, 2000b).

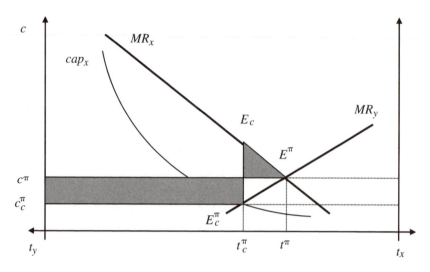

Figure 7.2   Payroll cap and owner profits

If the payroll cap is at the same time a floor, and some cross-subsidisation arrangements are in place, all clubs are forced to spend the same amount of money on playing talent. Given the existence of a cap, the two hyperbolic functions in Figure 7.1 are the new demand curves and the new market equilibrium is reached at their point of intersection with, obviously, a 50/50 distribution of talent and a lower salary level. The impact of this cap on the small-market club's profits is clearly positive, but it is theoretically unclear what happens to the profit of the large-market club, because the reduction in player salaries is smaller and the reduction in talent larger than without the floor (see Fort and Quirk, 1995). Total league revenue comes down again because of the inefficient allocation of talent.

Things get more complicated if one starts from the two-decision variable model, which is discussed in Chapter 4, where club owners have to decide simultaneously on the ticket price and the talent demand. In Figure 7.3, where the two decision variables are found on the axes, the first-order conditions for profit maximisation $\pi_t = 0$ and $\pi_p = 0$ are drawn. For the large-market club and an exogenously given salary level, a payroll cap can be drawn as a horizontal line $t = cap/c$ below the profit-maximising equilibrium point E^π. In a competitive player labour market, the salary level is not exogenous. We have to take into account that a lower demand for talent by the large-market clubs, and an unchanged demand for talent by the small-market club, will also lower the market-clearing salary level. This lower salary level will cause the cap line to shift upwards. However, the cap line

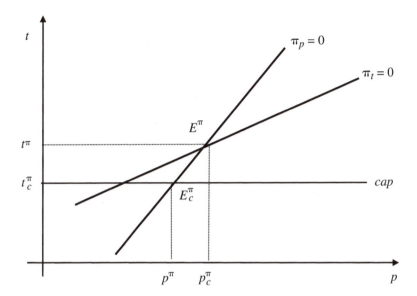

Figure 7.3   Payroll cap in a large-market club

stays below the competitive market equilibrium (given the fixed supply of talent, the market-clearing salary level cannot go down to a level that will increase the demand for talent by the large-market club because the small-market club's demand for talent goes up, as will be seen below). By this new horizontal line, the first-order condition $\pi_t = 0$ is no longer relevant. It follows that the optimal ticket price and talent demand is found in E_c^π at the point of intersection of the cap-line at t_c^π and the locus $\pi_p = 0$, which indicates a lower ticket price and a lower demand for talent by the large-market club.

If the payroll cap is a not a floor, it is not effective for the small-market club. There will only be an indirect effect caused by the lower equilibrium salary level in a competitive player market. Because this causes an upward shift of the locus $\pi_t = 0$, as seen in Figure 7.4, the new equilibrium is reached at the point of intersection E_c^π of the locus $\pi_p = 0$ and the shifted locus $\pi_t = 0$. It follows that both the ticket price and talent demand of the small club go up.

If the payroll cap is at the same time a floor, the small-market club is forced to spend more money on salaries with the extra money it receives from a cross-subsidisation programme. The cap line is now a horizontal line above the competitive market equilibrium in Figure 7.5, so the small-market club will increase its ticket price from p^π to p_c^π.

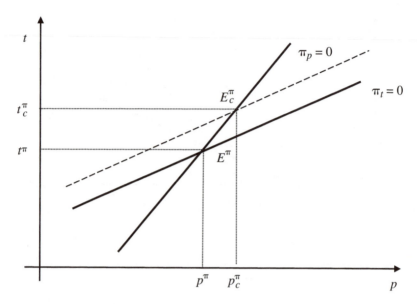

Figure 7.4   Payroll cap in a small-market club

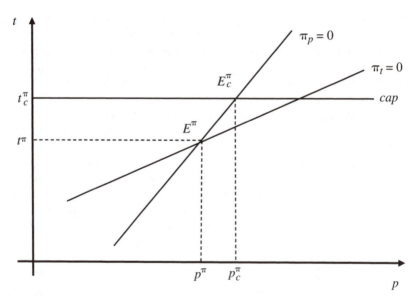

Figure 7.5   Payroll cap and floor in a small-market club

The conclusion is that a North American payroll cap, with or without a floor, improves the competitive balance and lowers the salary level in a profit-maximisation league. It has a different effect on the ticket price in large- and small-market clubs.

Numerical example

Returning to the numerical example of a two-decision-variable model in Chapter 4, and assuming that the large-market club's attendance function is:

$$A = \ln(1 + t) - p$$

with profit function:

$$\pi = p\ln(1 + t) - p^2 - ct$$

the first order conditions for profit maximisation $\pi_p = 0$ and $\pi_t = 0$, where subscripts indicate the partial derivatives, are:

$$p = \frac{\ln(1 + t)}{2}$$

$$p = c(1 + t).$$

Starting from a given salary level equal to 0.10, the free-market results are given for a number of variables in the first column of Table 7.1. One can see that the total payroll is 1.2. If we consider the case of a payroll cap of 1.0, which is not a floor and which is only relevant for this large-market club, and assuming further that the salary is exogenous and stays the same, the results are presented in the second column of Table 7.1. One can see now that, with the payroll staying below the cap, both the demand for

Table 7.1 Simulation results: North American salary cap

Large-market club	Free market equilibrium	Cap = 1.00 fixed salary	Cap = 1.00 lower salary
Salary level	0.10	0.10	0.09
Talents	12	10	11
Ticket price	1.30	1.10	1.08
Payroll	1.20	1.00	0.99
Attendance	1.26	1.29	1.40
Revenue	1.64	1.43	1.52
Profits	0.44	0.43	0.53

talents and the ticket price decrease. In this example, attendance is up because the positive effect of a lower ticket price is stronger than the negative effect of fewer talents. This result, however, is not generally true because it depends on the relative size of the price and talent elasticity of ticket demand. The same has to be said for total revenue and profits, which are going down in this example.

The last column presents the results under the more interesting assumption that the market-clearing salary level goes down from 0.10 to 0.09. The demand for talent and the ticket price are still lower compared to free market equilibrium. Attendance and total revenue are down but profits are up. What is important here is that, in both cases, the demand for talent and the ticket price are lower under the payroll cap, and that there is no guarantee that a payroll cap will increase profits in a two-decision variable model.

Individual salary cap
So far, we have not mentioned the possibility of imposing an individual salary cap. It goes without saying that imposing an individual cap, below the market equilibrium level, will create excess demand on the player labour market. So, some players can choose where to play, for the large- or for the small-market club. One can expect that most players will prefer to play for the richest club because this can provide more fringe benefits and greater exposure. As a consequence, an individual salary cap will probably worsen the competitive balance.

What if an individual salary cap is imposed together with a payroll cap (see Staudohar, 1999)? This is pictured in Figure 7.6, which can also be interpreted as a top-player model, as explained in section 3.3.3. The individual salary cap can be drawn as a horizontal line on the level of the individual cap (*capi*). It is obvious that, in order to be effective, this individual cap has to be lower than the salary level under the payroll cap in point E_c^{π}. Again the individual cap creates excess demand for top players. Given the new salary level $c = capi$, the new equilibrium point will be reached somewhere between the profit-maximising points of the large- and small-market clubs, but it can be expected again that players will prefer to play for the large-market club and the better team. If we compare the outcomes of a payroll cap with and without the individual cap, the profit-maximising large-market club will hire more top players with the individual cap. The small-market club is rationed and has to play with the players that are left over. It follows that the individual cap creates a more unbalanced competition. Moreover, the profits of the large-market club will be higher, whereas it is unclear what happens to the profits of the small-market club. One positive outcome of an individual cap is that it can improve the salary distribution between star players and regular players.

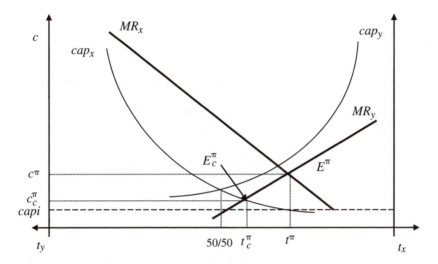

Figure 7.6   Individual salary cap and payroll cap

7.2.2   Win Maximisation

If clubs are win maximisers, the impact of a payroll cap, with or without the floor, will be very similar to the profit-maximisation case as presented in Figure 7.1, where the marginal revenue curves are simply to be replaced by the net average revenue curves. However, the motivation of the league administrators by imposing the cap can be different. If clubs are win maximisers, the payroll cap is not primarily meant to guarantee a reasonable profit rate, but rather to force clubs to maintain a sound financial structure. Again, the cap will lower the salary level and improve the competitive balance. The large-market club will become profitable, even if it is not interested in making profits. In a win-maximisation league, the payroll cap can increase total league revenue, because it moves the allocation of talent closer to the profit-maximisation equilibrium, where talent is more efficiently allocated.

In the two-decision-variable model, the impact of the payroll cap is presented in Figure 7.7 for a large-market club. Together with the first-order conditions, the zero-profit contour is also drawn. The club's initial equilibrium is given by point E^w, where talent is maximised given the zero-profit constraint. If a payroll cap is imposed, it can be represented again by a horizontal line below the equilibrium talent level. Now the large-market club has a choice: it can pocket the profits and move to the profit-maximising ticket price $p^{\pi 0}$, or it can maximise attendance under the zero-profit constraint by

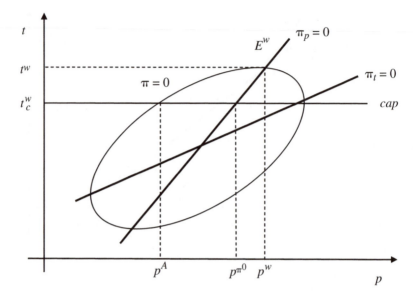

Figure 7.7   Payroll cap in a win-maximisation league, large-market club

lowering the ticket price to p^A. Of course, it can also choose to stay somewhere in between these two extreme positions. In any case, the ticket price of
the large-market club will be lower due to the payroll cap.

   If the payroll cap is also a floor, the small-market club, which receives a
subsidy, will increase its ticket price, as can be seen in Figure 7.8. The
subsidy allows the club to make a loss, so it can move outside the breakeven
contour $\pi = 0$ and, maximising talent, set the ticket price at p_c^w. If the
payroll cap is not a floor, the cap is not effective and the small-market club
is only affected indirectly. The cap causes a decrease of the equilibrium
salary level, so both the locus $\pi_t = 0$ and the breakeven contour $\pi = 0$ shift
upward and a higher ticket price is set (see Késenne and Pauwels, 2006).

7.3   SOFT CAP AND LUXURY TAX

In the previous section, it was assumed that the payroll cap was a hard
cap, which means that a club's payroll is not, under any circumstances,
allowed to exceed the value of the cap. However, in some North American
major leagues, soft salary caps are imposed. Clubs that pay more to their
players than the value of the cap have to pay a tax, which is often called a
luxury tax.

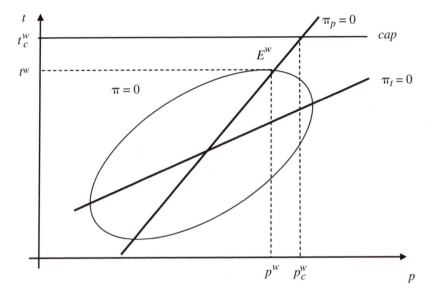

Figure 7.8 Payroll cap in a win-maximisation league, small-market club

Assume that a proportional tax is imposed on a club's payroll if the payroll exceeds the amount of the payroll cap. In this case, the profit function can be written as:

$$\pi_i = R[m_i, t_i] - (1 + \tau)ct_i \qquad \text{if} \qquad ct_i > cap.$$

The first-order condition for maximum profits is then:

$$\frac{\partial R_i}{\partial t_i} = c(1 + \tau).$$

If the tax is levied only on the high-budget clubs whose payroll exceeds the cap, then only the rich clubs will lower their demand for talent, so the distribution of talent improves.

In a two-club model where club x is the high-budget club, the market equilibrium is given by:

$$\frac{1}{1 + \tau} \frac{\partial R_x}{\partial t_x} = c = \frac{\partial R_y}{\partial t_y}$$

This improves the competitive balance compared with the pre-tax equilibrium. This can be illustrated in Figure 7.9, where the demand curve of the

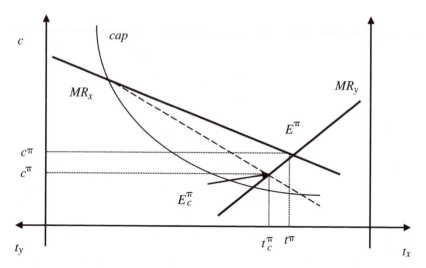

Figure 7.9   Luxury tax

large-market club is bent at the point where the payroll reaches the value of the cap. If the market equilibrium point before the luxury tax is imposed is E^{π}, the after-tax equilibrium point is E_c^{π}. The competitive balance improves and the salary level comes down.

A variant of this luxury tax is a progressive tax on season club revenue as proposed by Van de Burg and Prinz (2005), who show that it improves the distribution of talent. Although their proof starts from simplified match revenue functions, it can easily be shown that this result holds in general for a season revenue function that is concave in winning percentage or talent. Starting from the profit function $\pi_i = R_i[m_i, t_i] - ct_i - c_i^0$, the first-order condition for maximum profits, if a progressive tax rate τ_i on total club revenue is imposed, can be written as:

$$(1 - \tau_i)\frac{\partial R_i}{\partial t_i} = c \qquad \text{for all } i.$$

Comparing this equation with the first-order condition before taxation, and given the concavity of the revenue functions, it is obvious that the large-budget clubs will lower their demand for talent more than the low-budget clubs if the progressive tax rate τ_i is higher for the large-budget clubs. It follows that the competitive balance in the league improves. Obviously, given a constant supply of talent, the equilibrium salary level will come down.

Exactly the same results from imposing a luxury tax can be found under win maximisation.

7.4   G-14 PAYROLL CAP IN EUROPEAN FOOTBALL

The G-14, which is the union of the 18 (originally 14) most successful football clubs in Europe, has proposed a payroll cap that deviates fundamentally from the North American cap in (7.1). The proposal, which is only a gentlemen's agreement, is to fix a maximum wage/turnover ratio or:

$$\frac{ct_i}{R_i} \le \alpha, \qquad \text{so} \quad cap_i = \alpha R_i \quad \text{with} \quad \alpha < 1. \qquad (7.2)$$

where α is a fixed wage/turnover ratio. Unlike the North American cap, the maximum amount that a club can spend on player salaries is different for each club, so a different impact on competitive balance and salary level can also be expected.

Starting with **profit maximisation**, the G-14 salary cap shows some resemblance to the macroeconomic proposal of Weitzman (1984) to fight stagflation, which he called the 'share economy'. An implication of Weitzman's labour compensation system, which gives workers a percentage of a firm's revenue, is that the marginal revenue of labour is always higher than the marginal cost. Based on the payroll cap in (7.2), $MC_i = \alpha MR_i$ and the profit function can be written as:

$$\pi_i = (1 - \alpha)R_i - c_i^0,$$

so all profit-maximising clubs are willing to hire talent until the marginal revenue of playing talent is zero. If all playing talent is looking for the best-paying team, it can be shown that this type of salary cap worsens the competitive balance. If the G-14 payroll cap is binding for both the large- and small-market clubs, the new market equilibrium is found at the point of intersection of the AR curves:

$$\frac{\alpha R_i}{t_i} = c \qquad \text{or} \qquad AR_i = c/\alpha \qquad \text{for all } i. \qquad (7.3)$$

It follows that the profit-maximisation equilibrium under a G-14 salary cap results in the same equilibrium as in a win-maximisation league (in the absence of any capital compensation). As can be seen in Figure 3.3, which is repeated here in Figure 7.10, this will cause a more unequal distribution of talent compared with the market equilibrium in a profit-maximisation league. However, the salary level that emerges after the introduction of the payroll cap is not found at the point of intersection of the AR curves, because the payroll is only a fixed percentage α of the average revenue.

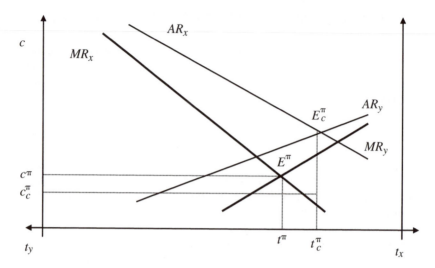

Figure 7.10   G-14 payroll cap in a profit-maximisation league (a)

Given the main objective of the G-14 cap, the parameter α will be set low enough to be effective. In Figure 7.10, the new unit cost of talent, or salary level, is given by c_c^π.

Using the quadratic revenue functions $R_i = m_i t_i - \beta t_i^2$ in a two-club model with $m_x > m_y$, the more unequal distribution of talent under a G-14 cap can be calculated as, referring to the results found in Chapter 3:

$$t_x^w - t_y^w = \frac{(m_x - m_y)}{\beta} > t_x^\pi - t_y^\pi = \frac{(m_x - m_y)}{2\beta}.$$

The player salary level can then be calculated as:

$$c_c^\pi = \frac{\alpha R_i}{t_i} = \alpha(m_i - bt_i).$$

This result is based on the fact that the payroll cap is binding for both clubs. It is possible, however, that the G-14 cap is not binding for the large-market club.

With the quadratic revenue functions, it can be derived that the small-market club has a larger wage/turnover ratio than the large-market club. Using the solutions derived in Chapter 3, one finds that:

$$\frac{ct_x^\pi}{R_x} = \frac{4c^\pi}{3m_x + m_y - 2\beta} < \frac{ct_y^\pi}{R_y} = \frac{4c^\pi}{3m_y + m_x - 2\beta}.$$

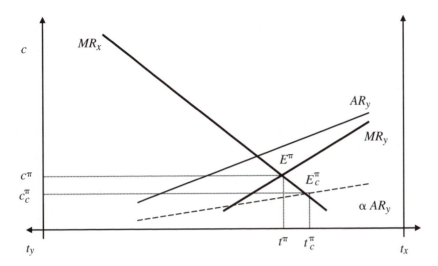

Figure 7.11 G-14 payroll cap in a profit-maximisation league (b)

If the payroll cap is not relevant for the large-market club but only affects the payroll of the small-market club, the result is also a more unbalanced distribution of playing talent, as can be seen from Figure 7.11. The large-market club's demand curve for talent is still given by the marginal revenue curve MR_x while the small-market club's demand is given by the curve αAR_y. The new market equilibrium is found at the point of intersection E_c^π, which also gives a more unequal distribution of talent. One can conclude that a G-14 payroll cap worsens the competitive balance in a profit-maximisation league.

Because the G-14 salary cap is only a gentlemen's agreement, Dietl, Franck and Nüesch (2006) have investigated under what conditions such a voluntary salary cap agreement is self-enforcing. Based on their theoretical model, the clubs' valuation of future profits and the importance of competitive balance for public interest add to the self-enforcing character.

In a **win-maximisation** league, where a club's demand for talent is given by the net average revenue curve (*NAR*), the free market equilibrium is found where:

$$NAR_i = \frac{R_i - c_i^0}{t_i} = c \qquad \text{for all } i.$$

If the G-14 cap is imposed, and if the cap is relevant for both clubs, the market equilibrium is given by (7.3), so both equilibria can be compared.

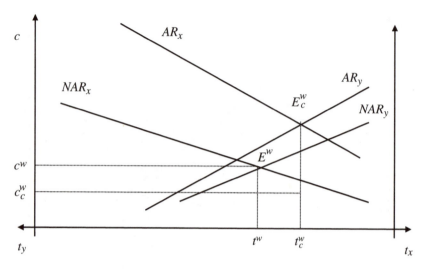

Figure 7.12   G-14 payroll cap in a win-maximisation league

Different outcomes are possible now, depending on the size of the fixed capital cost.

If the capital cost is assumed to be proportional to total revenue with proportionality factor k:

$$c_i^0 = kR_i, \quad \text{so} \quad NAR_i = (1-k)AR_i,$$

the distribution of talent, as well as the wage–turnover ratios, will be the same as before. However, if the proportionality factor k is larger for the large-market club, the G-14 cap worsens the competitive balance in a win-maximisation league. This can be seen by considering the shifts of the demand curves of the large- and small-market clubs in Figure 7.12. If the free market equilibrium is given by E^w, the point of intersection of net average revenue curves, the equilibrium after the introduction of the payroll cap is point E_c^w. Given the higher value of k in the large-market club, the NAR curve of the large-market club is flatter. It follows that the G-14 salary cap will also worsen the competitive balance in a win-maximisation league. Given that the major concern of the G-14 is the sound financial structure of the European football clubs, the point of reference for analysing the impact of a payroll cap is not the breakeven point of all clubs. If the financial losses of the small-market clubs are, on average, larger than those of the large-market clubs, it is obvious that in this case also the G-14 payroll cap worsens the competitive balance (see Késenne, 2003).

7.5 CONCLUSION

All problems of enforcing salary caps aside, one can conclude that the North American style of payroll cap, which imposes the same maximum amount on all clubs, has a favourable effect on competitive balance. It also lowers the labour cost of clubs, which helps professional teams located in weak-drawing markets to maintain financial viability. In general, a salary cap will not bring ticket prices down. Small-market clubs, whether they are profit or win maximisers, can be expected to increase their ticket prices. If the cap is also a floor, it is not guaranteed that a salary cap will increase the large-market clubs' profits.

The G-14 type of payroll cap, which fixes a maximum turnover ratio, and thus the amount of the cap is different for each team, can be expected to worsen the competitive balance. But it does reach its major objective, which is to restore the troubled financial structure of many clubs.

EXERCISES 7

7.1. Starting from the revenue functions $R_x = 160t_x - 100t_x^2$ and $R_x = 120t_y - 100t_y^2$, with $t_x + t_y = 1$, the profit-maximisation equilibrium is $t_x^\pi / t_y^\pi = 0.6/0.4 = 1.5$ and $c^\pi = 40$. The payroll of the large-market club is then 24 and of the small-market club 16. Assuming that a payroll cap of 20 is imposed by the league, what will the distribution of talent and the salary level be?

7.2. Starting from the same profit-maximisation model as in exercise 7.1, and assuming that a soft salary cap is fixed at 20, and that the large market club, exceeding the value of the cap, has to pay a luxury tax rate of $\tau = 0.1$, what will the distribution of talent and the salary level be?

7.3. Starting again from the same profit-maximisation model as in exercise 7.1:
  - Calculate the wage turnover ratio of both clubs.
  - If the league is imposing a maximum value of the wage–turnover ratio of 30 per cent, what will the new market equilibrium distribution of talent and the salary level be?

7.4. Starting again from the same profit-maximisation model as in exercise 7.1, and assuming that the maximum wage–turnover ratio is fixed at 45 per cent and thus not binding for the large-market club, derive the equilibrium distribution of talent and the salary level.

7.5. With the same revenue functions as in exercise 7.1, but now with win-maximising clubs, assume that for the capital cost of both clubs it holds that $c_i^0 = 0.20R_i$. If a maximum wage–turnover ratio of 60 per cent is imposed, what will the equilibrium distribution of talent and the salary level be?

Answers to exercises

EXERCISES 1

1.1. A profit-maximising club will hire talent until marginal revenue equals marginal cost:

$$\partial R/\partial t = 10 - 2t = \partial C/\partial t = 2, \quad \text{so} \quad t_1 = 4.$$

Profits are $\pi_1 = R_1 - C_1 = 24 - 8 = 16$.

1.2. A revenue-maximising club will hire talents until marginal revenue is zero:

$$\partial R/\partial t = 10 - 2t = 0, \quad \text{so} \quad t_2 = 5.$$

The club is still profitable, $\pi_2 = R_2 - C_2 = 25 - 10 = 15$.

1.3. A win-maximising club, under the breakeven condition, will hire talent until total revenue equals total cost. $R = 10t - t^2 = C = 2t$ so the quadratic equation $8t - t^2 = 0$ has to be solved. This equation has two solutions, $t_4 = 8$ and $t_4' = 0$. A win-maximising club will obviously choose the first solution. One can check that profits are indeed zero, $\pi_4 = R_4 - C_4 = 16 - 16 = 0$.

1.4. If a linear combination of profits and wins $\pi + at$ is maximised with $a = 3$, the first-order condition is $11 - 2t = 0$, so $t_3 = 5.5$ and $\pi_3 = R_5 - C_5 = 24.75 - 11 = 13.75$.

EXERCISES 2

2.1. If the club owner's objective is to make as much profit as possible, the optimality condition is given by $\partial R/\partial p = \partial C/\partial p = 0$. If total revenue is $R = pA = 5p - 0.5p^2$ the optimality condition is $\partial R/\partial p = 5 - p = 0$, so the optimal ticket price is 5 Euro and attendance is 25 000. Total revenue is 125 000. However, if the stadium can only accommodate

20 000 spectators, the manager will set the price at 6 Euro by solving $2 = 5 - 0.5p$. Total revenue is 120 000.

2.2. The optimality condition for profit maximisation with $R = (p+4)A = 20 + 3p - 0.5p^2$ is now $\partial R/\partial p = 3 - p = 0$, so the optimal ticket price is 3 Euro and attendance is 35 000. Total revenue is $7 \times 135\,000 = 245\,000$. If the stadium can only take 20 000 fans, the manager will again set the price at 6 Euro. Total revenue is now $10 \times 20\,000 = 200\,000$.

2.3. Given the inverse ticket demand function $p = 10 - 2A$, and a maximum ticket price of 2, the number of spectators can be found by solving $2 = 10 - 2A$, so $A = 40\,000$ and club revenue is 80 000.

2.4. Table A1 presents the club's profits for every ticket price and every unit cost of talent. One observes that, whatever the cost of talent, the ticket price that maximises profit is always the same: $p = 5$. What this simple numerical example shows is that the unit cost of talent or the players' salary level does not affect the profit-maximising ticket price. Note that profit maximisation also means loss minimisation if there is no ticket price that makes the club profitable.

Table A1   Answer to exercise 2.4

p	A	R	$c = 2$		$c = 3$		$c = 4$	
			C	π	C	π	C	π
3	3.5	10.5	8	2.5	12	−1.5	16	−5.5
4	3	12	8	4	12	0	16	−4
5	2.5	12.5	8	4.5	12	0.5	16	−3.5
6	2	12	8	4	12	0	16	−4
7	1.5	10.5	8	2.5	12	−1.5	16	−5.5

2.5. Because total revenue is given by $R = 12q_r - 2q_r^2$, the marginal revenue is $\partial R/\partial q_r = 12 - 4q_r$. With a marginal cost that is zero, the optimality condition is given by: $12 - 4q_r = 0$, so $q_{r1} = 3$ and $p_{r1} = 6$. Total revenue $R_t = 18$ and profit $\pi_1 = 15$.

2.6. In a competitive market of TV rights, the equilibrium is found where demand equals supply. The supply curve, being the marginal cost curve, is $p_r = 0.4q_r$. It follows that the optimum is found where $12 - 2q_r = 0.4q_r$, so $q_{r2} = 5$ and $p_{r2} = 2$. Total revenue $R_2 = 10$, total cost $C_2 = 7$ and profit $\pi_2 = 3$. Comparing these results with the previous ones, league profits are much lower, so the league and the clubs are better off under pooling, but the price is much lower and the output higher, so the spectators are better off under decentralised selling in a competitive market.

2.7. The total revenue of the broadcast company can be found to be $R = pq + R_a = 14q_s - 0.5q_s^2$, so the first-order condition is: $MR = 14 - q_s = MC = 0$ and $q_{s1} = 14$ and $p_{s1} = 3$. The revenue from advertising is 56; the revenue from viewing is 42. Total revenue is 98 so the total profit is 48. In the case of free-to-air broadcasting, the price is zero and the number of spectators will be 20. Although revenue from advertising is now 80, which is higher then under pay-per-view, it is also the only revenue source, so total profit is 30. We can derive that the company will choose pay-per-view. Obviously, the spectator would prefer the free-to-air broadcasting of games.

EXERCISES 3

3.1. Under profit maximisation the player market equilibrium can be found from: $160 - 200t_x = 120 - 200(1 - t_x)$, which results in: $t_x^\pi = 0.6$ and $t_y^\pi = 0.4$ or $(w_x^\pi/w_y^\pi) = 1.5$. The market-clearing unit cost of talent, which is equal to the marginal revenue in both clubs, can be calculated as $c_\pi = 40$. The total revenue of club x is then equal to: $R_x^\pi = 160(0.6) - 100(0.6)^2 = 60$. The total revenue of club y is: $R_y^\pi = 120(0.4) - 100(0.4)^2 = 32$, so the total league revenue is: $R^\pi = 60 + 32 = 92$. The profits of club x are: $\pi_x = 60 - 40(0.6) = 36$. The profits of club y are: $\pi_y = 32 - 0.4(40) = 16$.

3.2. Under win maximisation the player market equilibrium can be found from $160 - 100t_x = 120 - 100(1 - t_x)$, which results in: $t_x^w = 0.7$ and $t_y^w = 0.3$ or $w_x^w/w_y^w = 2.33$. The competitive balance is more unequal than in a profit-maximisation league. The market clearing unit cost of talent, which is equal to the average revenue in both clubs, can be calculated as $c_w = 90$, which is higher than under profit maximisation. The total revenue of club x is then equal to: $R_x^w = 160(0.7) - 100(0.7)^2 = 63$. The total revenue of club y is: $R_y^w = 120(0.3) - 100(0.3)^2 = 27$, so the total league revenue is $R^w = 63 + 27 = 90$, showing that win maximisation causes a loss of total league revenue of $R^\pi - R^w = 92 - 90 = 2$.

3.3. Based on the equation derived in section 3.4, $t_i^w = 2t_i^\pi - 0.5$, which also applies to the winning percentages, this can be calculated as listed

Table A2   Answer to exercise 3.3

w_i^π	$w_i^w = 2w_i^\pi - 0.5$
0.70	0.90
0.60	0.70
0.55	0.60
0.50	0.50
0.35	0.20
0.30	0.10
3.00	3.00

in Table A2. It is clear that the standard deviation of the win percentages in the win-maximisation league is larger than the standard deviation in the profit-maximisation league.

3.4. Under these conditions the result can be found from: $160 - 200t_x = 120 - 100(1 - t_x)$, so $t_x^{\pi w} = 0.47$ and $t_y^{\pi w} = 0.53$ and $c_{\pi w} = 67$.

3.5. If the small-market club is more win orientated than the large-market club, the result can be found from: $160 - 200t_x = 120 - 200(1 - t_x) + 40$, so $t_x = 0.5$ and $t_y = 0.5$ and $c = 60$.

3.6. Under win maximisation the player market equilibrium can then be derived from:

$$NAR_x = 160 - 100t_x - \frac{20}{t_x} = NAR_y = 120 - 100(1 - t_x).$$

The distribution of talent can then be found from the solution of the quadratic function:

$$200t_x^2 - 140t_x + 20 = 0, \text{ so } t_x^w = \frac{140 \pm (140^2 - 4(200 \times 20))}{2 \times 200}$$

$$= 0.5 \text{ and } t_y^w = 0.5.$$

The unit cost of talent $c = 70$. One observes that the distribution of talent can be more equal in a win-maximisation league compared with a profit-maximisation league if the differences in the fixed capital cost are large enough.

3.7. If the negative external effects, due to the constant talent supply, are not internalised, the teams' demand curves are given by the quadratic functions: $2bt_i^2 - (m_i + 2b)t_i + m_i = c$, so the following equation should be solved for t_x: $200t_x^2 - 360t_x + 160 = c = 200 (1 - t_x)^2 - 320(1 - t_x) + 120$. After some rearrangements, this reduces to solving $160 - 360t_x = 0$, so $t_x^\pi = 160/280 = 0.57$, yielding the competitive balance $w_x^\pi/w_y^\pi = 1.33$. Given that $w_x^\pi + w_y^\pi = 1$, the winning percentages are $w_x^\pi = 0.57$ and $w_y^\pi = 0.43$. The salary level can then be found to be $c^\pi = 19.5$. The competitive balance in the flexible-supply Nash equilibrium is given by the ratio of the market sizes, $w_x^\pi/w_y^\pi = m_x/m_y = 160/120 = 1.33$, for any salary level. The competitive balance in the case of a constant-supply Walras equilibrium is $t_x^\pi/t_y^\pi = 1.5$ with salary level $c^\pi = 40$.

EXERCISES 4

4.1. The unconstrained profit-maximising equilibrium is found at the point of intersection of the two first-order conditions:

$$\frac{\partial \pi}{\partial t} = \frac{p}{4\sqrt{t}} - 1 = 0$$

$$\frac{\partial \pi}{\partial p} = \frac{\sqrt{t}}{2} = 0$$

which results in $t^* = 4$ and $p^* = 8$. The ticket price is above the maximum ticket price, so the new equilibrium is found at the point of intersection of the locus $\pi_t = 0$ and the ticket price constraint: $6/(4\sqrt{t}) = 1$ so $t^{**} = 2.25$.

4.2. In this case, the optimal ticket price and the hiring of talent can be found at the point of intersection of the price line and the stadium capacity constraint. The stadium capacity constraint can be written as: $t = p^2/4$ or $p = 2\sqrt{t}$, so the optimum is found where: $2\sqrt{t} = 8$, so $t^* = 16$.

EXERCISES 5

5.1. The equilibrium of a non-discriminating profit-maximising monopsonist is found by the solution of: $MR = 2.8 - 2t = MC = 0.4 + t$, so $t_m^\pi = 0.8$. Using the supply function, the salary level can be found as $c_m^\pi = 0.8$. The marginal revenue $MR_m^\pi = 1.2$, so the rate of monopsonistic exploitation (RME) can be calculated as $RME = 1 - c_m^\pi/MR_m^\pi = 0.33$.

5.2. The equilibrium of a discriminating profit-maximising monopsonist is found by $MR = 2.8 - 2t = MC = 0.4 + 0.5t$, so $t_{dm}^{\pi} = 0.96$. All playing talents are paid a different salary level.

5.3. The equilibrium demand for talent of win-maximising non-discriminating and discriminating monopsonists will be the same and can be found by solving $AR = 2.8 - t = AC = 0.4 + 0.5t$, so $t_m^w = 1.6$. If the monopsonist does not discriminate, he pays every talent: $c_m^w = 1.2$. This is above marginal revenue, which can even be negative: $MR_m^w = -0.4$. It is possible that a win-maximising club may hire a talent with a negative marginal revenue.

EXERCISES 6

6.1. The revenue functions after sharing can be written as:

$$R_x^* = 0.8R_x + 0.2R_y \qquad \text{and} \qquad R_y^* = 0.8R_y + 0.2R_x.$$

The corresponding marginal revenues are then, knowing that $t_x + t_y = 1$:

$$MR_x^* = 0.8(160 - 200t_x) - 0.2(120 - 200t_y) = 144 - 200t_x$$

$$MR_y^* = 0.8(120 - 200t_y) - 0.2(160 - 200t_x) = 104 - 200t_y.$$

The market equilibrium, or the point of intersection of the two demand curves for talent after sharing, is found by the solution of $144 - 200t_x = 104 - 200(1 - t_x)$, so $t_x^* = 0.6$ and $t_y^* = 0.4$, which is the same as the distribution of talent before sharing. The salary level $c^* = 144 - 200(0.6) = 24$, which is lower than the salary level before sharing.

6.2. Table A3 presents the main results for the three values of the share parameter; if $\mu = 1$, there is no sharing, if $\mu = 0$, there is equal sharing. One can see that revenue sharing increases the poor club's profits. It decreases the rich club's profits because they are larger than the average budget in the league. Total league profits go up due to the sharing arrangement. It can also be seen that the distribution of talent before sharing ($\mu = 1$) is the same as after sharing according to the invariance proposition. Bear in mind that a pool share parameter of $\mu = 0.5$ means that the large club keeps 75 per cent of its revenue and receives 25 per cent of the small clubs' revenue. If $\mu = 0$, which means equal sharing,

Table A3   Answer to exercise 6.2

μ	t_x/t_y	R_x	R_y	$\bar{R}$	c	C_x	C_y	π_x	π_y	π
1	8/2	96	12	54	40	32	8	64	4	68
0.5	8/2	75	33	54	20	16	4	59	29	88
0	8/2	54	54	54	0	0	0	54	54	108

all clubs' revenues and profits are equal, and the market-clearing unit cost of talent is zero; clubs are no longer willing to pay for talent.

6.3. After sharing, the average revenue functions are:

$$AR_x^* = 160 - 100t_x - \tfrac{1}{2}(160 - 140) = 150 - 100t_x$$

$$AR_y^* = 120 - 100t_y - \tfrac{1}{2}(120 - 140) = 130 - 100t_y,$$

so under win maximisation a more equal distribution of talent is reached, $t_x^*/t_y^* = 0.6/0.4$. We know that this also maximises total league revenue. (why?) Under profit maximisation, the distribution of talent becomes: $t_x^*/t_y^* = 0.55/0.45$.

6.4. Equalising the two marginal revenue curves after sharing:

$$0.5(m_x - 2bt_x)t_y - 0.5(m_y - 2bt_y)t_y = 0.5(m_y - 2bt_y)t_x$$
$$- 0.5(m_x - 2bt_x)t_x,$$

which can be simplified to:

$$m_xt_x - m_yt_y + 2bt_y^2 = m_yt_x - m_xt_x + 2bt_x^2$$

or $m_x - m_y = 2b(t_x^2 - t_y^2)$,

so $t_x - t_y = \dfrac{m_x - m_y}{2b}$.

EXERCISES 7

7.1. Because the salary cap is only relevant for the large-market club, the new equilibrium is found as the solution of: $20/t_x = 120 - 200t_y$, so the following quadratic function has to be solved: $200t_x^2 - 80t_x - 20 = 0$.

The solution is $t_x^c = (80 + \sqrt{(6400 + 4(4000)))}/400 = 0.57$, so $t_x^c/t_y^c = 0.57/0.43 = 1.32$, which is a more equal competitive balance. The new salary level is $c^c = 20/0.57 = 35$, which is lower.

7.2. The new equilibrium can be found by the solution of: $(1 - 0.1)(160 - 200t_x) = 120 - 200t_y$, so $t_x^c = 0.59$, so $t_x^c/t_y^c = 0.59/0.41 = 1.44$. The salary level is then $c^c = 0.38$.

7.3. The wage–turnover ratio can be calculated for the large- and the small-market club as $c_\pi t_x^\pi/R_x^\pi = 0.4$ and $c_\pi t_y^\pi/R_y^\pi = 0.5$. If the maximum turnover ratio is 0.3, the new market equilibrium can be found as the solution of $0.3AR_x = 0.3AR_y$ or $160 - 100t_x = 120 - 100(1 - t_x)$, so $t_x^c/t_y^c = 0.7/0.3 = 2.3$ and $c^c = 0.3(160 - 70) = 27$. One can verify that, in this equilibrium, the wage–turnover ratios of both clubs are equal at 0.3.

7.4. In this case the demand for talent of the profit-maximising large-market club is given by the marginal revenue. The new market equilibrium is then found as the solution of:

$$MR_x = 0.45AR_y \text{ or } 160 - 200t_x = 0.45(120 - 100(1 - t_x)),$$

so $t_x^c/t_y^c = 0.62/0.38 = 1.63$ and $c^c = 1.6 - 2(0.62) = 0.36$. In this case, the wage–turnover ratio of the small-market club is 0.45. The wage–turnover ratio of the large-market club is 0.36.

7.5. In a free market, the distribution of talent is found by solving $NAR_x = NAR_y$: $(1 - 0.20)AR_x = (1 - 0.20)AR_y$, so $t_x^c/t_y^c = 0.7/0.3 = 2.3$. This talent distribution is not affected by imposing a G-14 cap, because the capital cost is proportional to club revenue, and the solution with the cap is given by $AR_x = AR_y$, which is obviously the same as without the cap. The free-market salary level is $c^w = (1 - 0.20)AR^w = (1 - 0.20)90 = 72$. With this salary level, the wage–turnover ratios, which are the same in both clubs for obvious reasons, are equal to:

$$\frac{c^w t_x^w}{R_x^w} = \frac{50.4}{63} = \frac{c^w t_y^w}{R_y^w} = \frac{21.6}{27} = 0.8.$$

Because this is too high, the salary level has been brought down to $c^c = 0.60AR^w = 0.60(90) = 54$.

References and selected bibliography

Akerlof, G. and J. Yellen (1986), *Efficiency Wage Models of the Labor Market*, Cambridge: Cambridge University Press.

Alexander, D. (2001), 'Major League Baseball: Monopoly Pricing and Profit Maximising Behavior', *Journal of Sports Economics*, 2 (4), 356–68.

Andreff, W. (1989), *Economie Politique du Sport*, Paris: Editions Dalloz.

Andreff, W. and S. Szymanski (2006), *Handbook of Sports Economics*, Cheltenham, UK and Northampton, MA, US: Edward Elgar.

Atkinson, S., L. Stanley and J. Tschirhart (1988), 'Revenue Sharing as an Incentive in an Agency Problem: An Example from the National Football League', *RAND Journal of Economics*, 19 (1), 27–43.

Baade, R. (1996), 'Professional Sports as Catalists for Metropolitan Economic Development', *Journal of Urban Affairs*, 18 (1), 1–17.

Barros, C., M. Ibrahimo and S. Szymanski (eds) (2002), *Transatlantic Sports: The Comparative Economics of North American and European Sports*, Cheltenham, UK and Northampton, MA, US: Edward Elgar.

Borghans, L. and L. Groot (2005), *The Competition Balance on Team Quality*, Working paper, Utrecht School of Economics, University of Utrecht.

Borland, J. and R. Macdonald (2003), 'Demand for Sport', *Oxford Review of Economic Policy*, 19 (4), 478–503.

Bourg, J.-F. and J.-J. Gouguet (1998), *Analyse Economique du Sport*, Paris: Presses Universitaires de France.

Cairns, J., N. Jennett and P. Sloane (1986), 'The Economics of Professional Team Sports: A Survey of Theory and Evidence', *Journal of Economic Studies*, 13 (1), 3–80.

Coase, R. (1960), 'The Problem of Social Cost', *Journal of Law and Economics*, 3, 1–44.

Dabscheck, B. (1975), 'Sporting Equality: Labour Market versus Product Market Control', *Journal of Industrial Relations*, 17 (2), 174–90.

Demmert, H. (1973), *The Economics of Professional Team Sports*, Lexington, MA: Lexington Books.

Dietl, H., E. Franck and S. Nüesch (2006), 'Are Voluntary Salary Cap Agreements Self-Enforcing?', *European Sport Management Quarterly*, 6 (1), 23–34.

Dobson, S. and J. Goddard (2001), *The Economics of Football*, Cambridge: Cambridge University Press.

Downward, P. and A. Dawson (2000), *The Economics of Professional Team Sports*, London and New York: Routledge.

El-Hodiri, M. and J. Quirk (1971), 'An Economic Model of a Professional Sports League', *Journal of Political Economy*, 79, 1302–19.

European Court of Justice (1995), *Union royale belge des sociétés de football association ASBL v Jean-Marc Bosman, Royal club liégeois SA v Jean-Marc Bosman and others and Union des associations européennes de football (UEFA) v Jean-Marc Bosman*. Case C-415/93, European Court reports 1995 Page I-04921. http://eur-lex.europa.eu/LexUriServ/LexUriServ.do?uri=CELEX:61993J0415:EN:HTML, accessed 22 December 2006.

Feess, E. and G. Muehlheusser (2003a), 'Transfer Fee Regulations in European Football', *European Economic Review*, 47, 645–68.

Feess, E. and G. Muehlheusser (2003b), 'The Impact of Transfer Fees on Professional Sports: An Analysis of the New Transfer System for European Football', *Scandinavian Journal of Economics*, 105 (1), 139–54.

FIFA–EU Transfer Agreement (2001), Brussels: European Commission.

Ferguson, D., K. Stewart, J. Jones and A. Le Dressay (1991), 'The Pricing of Sport Events: Do Teams Maximize Profits?' *Journal of Industrial Economics*, 39 (3), 297–310.

Fizel, J. (ed.) (2006), *Handbook of Sports Economics Research*, London: M.E. Sharp.

Fizel, J., L. Gustafson and J. Hadley (eds) (1996), *Baseball Economics, Current Research*, Westport, CT: Greenwood Press.

Fizel, J., L. Gustafson and J. Hadley (eds) (1999), *Sports Economics, Current Research*, London: Praeger.

Forrest, D. and R. Simmons (2002), 'Outcome Uncertainty and Attendance Demand in Sport: The Case of English Soccer', *The Statistician*, 51 (2), 229–41.

Fort, R. (2003), *Sports Economics*, Englewood Cliffs, NJ: Prentice Hall.

Fort, R. and J. Fizel (eds) (2004), *International Sports Economics Comparisons*, Westport: Praeger Publishers.

Fort, R. and J. Quirk (1995), 'Cross-subsidization, Incentives and Outcomes in Professional Team Sports Leagues', *Journal of Economic Literature*, 33 (3), 1265–99.

Fort, R. and J. Quirk (2004), 'Owner Objectives and Competitive Balance', *Journal of Sports Economics*, 5 (1), 20–32.

Frick, B. (2003), 'Contest Theory and Sport', *Oxford Review of Economic Policy*, 19 (4), 512–29.

Garcia, J. and P. Rodriguez (2002), 'The Determinants of Football Match Attendance Revisited: Empirical Evidence from the Spanish Football League', *Journal of Sports Economics*, 3 (1), 18–38.

Gerrard, B. (ed.) (2006), *The Economics of Association Football*, Cheltenham, UK and Northampton, MA, US: Edward Elgar.

Goossens, K. (2006), *National Measure of Seasonal Imbalance for Team Sports*, Discussion paper, Economics Department, University of Antwerp.

Goossens, K. and S. Késenne (2007), 'National Dominance in European Football Leagues', in T. Slack and M. Parent (eds), *International Perspectives on the Management of Sport*, Burlington, MA: Elsevier (forthcoming).

Gratton, C. and P. Taylor (2000), *Economics of Sport and Recreation*, London: Spon Press.

Haan, M., R. Koning and A. van Witteloostuijn (2005), *Institutional Change in European Soccer: A Theoretical Analysis of the Effects on Competitive Balance and the Quality of National Competitions*, Discussion paper, Department of Economics, University of Groningen.

Hendricks, W. (ed.) (1997), *Advances in the Economics of Sport*, Vol. 2, Greenwich: JAI Press.

Hoehn, T. and S. Szymanski (1999), 'The Americanisation of European Football', *Economic Policy*, 28 (April), 207–40.

Humphreys, B. (2002), 'Alternative Measures of Competitive Balance', *Journal of Sports Economics*, 3 (2), 133–48.

Janssens, P. and S. Késenne (1987), 'Belgian Soccer Attendances', *Tijdschrift voor Economie en Management*, 32, 305–15.

Jeanrenaud, C. and S. Késenne (eds) (1999), *Competition Policy in Professional Sports*, Antwerp: Standaard Editions Ltd.

Jeanrenaud, C. and S. Késenne (eds) (2006), *Sports and the Media*, Cheltenham, UK and Northampton, MA, US: Edward Elgar.

Jennett, N. (1984), 'Attendances, Uncertainty of Outcome and Policy in the Scottish Football League', *Scottish Journal of Political Economy*, 31 (2), 176–98.

Jones, J. (1969), 'The Economics of the National Hockey League', *Canadian Journal of Economics*, 2 (1), 1–20.

Kahane, L. (2006), 'The Reverse-Order-of-Finish Draft in Sports', in W. Andreff and S. Szymanski (eds), *Handbook of Sports Economics*, Cheltenham, UK and Northampton, MA, US: Edward Elgar.

Késenne, S. (1996), 'League Management in Professional Team Sports with Win Maximizing Clubs', *European Journal for Sports Management*, 2 (2), 14–22.

Késenne, S. (2000a), 'Revenue Sharing and Competitive Balance in Professional Team Sports', *Journal of Sports Economics*, 1 (1), 56–65.

Késenne, S. (2000b), 'The Impact of Salary Caps in Professional Team Sports', *Scottish Journal of Political Economy*, 47 (4), 431–55.

Késenne, S. (2003), 'The Salary Cap Proposal of the G-14 in European Football', *European Sports Management Quarterly*, 3 (2), 120–28.

Késenne, S. (2005), 'Revenue Sharing and Competitive Balance: Does the Invariance Proposition Hold?' *Journal of Sports Economics*, 6 (1), 98–106.

Késenne, S. (2006), 'The Win Maximisation Model Reconsidered', *Journal of Sports Economics*, 7 (4), 416–27.

Késenne, S. (2007a), 'Revenue Sharing and Owner Profits', *Journal of Sports Economics* (forthcoming).

Késenne, S. (2007b), 'The Peculiar International Economics of Professional Team Sports', *Scottish Journal of Political Economy* (forthcoming).

Késenne, S. and W. Pauwels (2006), 'Club Objectives and Ticket Pricing in Professional Team Sports', *Eastern Economic Journal*, 32 (3), 549–60.

Koning, R. (2003), 'An Econometric Evaluation of the Effect of Firing a Coach on Team Performance', *Journal of Applied Economics*, 35 (5), 555–64.

Krautmann, A. and L. Hadley (2004), 'Of Dynasties and Dogs', paper presented at the Sixth International Conference of the International Association of Sports Economists, Athens, Greece, 31 May–2 June.

Kringstad, M. and B. Gerrard (2007), 'Beyond Competitive Balance', in T. Slack and M. Parent (eds), *International Perspectives on the Management of Sport*, Burlington, MA: Elsevier (forthcoming).

Lavoie, M. (2000), 'La Proposition d'Invariance dans un Monde où les Equipes Maximisent la Performance Sportive', *Réflets et Perspectives de la vie Economique*, 39 (2–3), 85–94.

Leeds, M. and P. Von Allmen (2002), *The Economics of Sports*, Boston: Addison-Wesley.

Longley, N. (1995), 'Salary Discrimination in the National Hockey League: the Effects of Team Location', *Canadian Public Policy*, 21 (4), 413–22.

Marburger, D. (1997a), 'Gate Revenue Sharing and Luxury Taxes in Professional Sports', *Contemporary Economic Policy*, 15 (April), 114–23.

Marburger, D. (ed.) (1997b), *Stee-Rike Four! What's Wrong with the Business of Baseball?* Westport: Praeger.

Markham, J. and P. Teplitz (1981), *Beseball Economics and Public Policy*, Lexington, MA: Lexington Books.

Neale, W. (1964), 'The Peculiar Economics of Professional Sports', *Quarterly Journal of Economics*, 78 (1), 1–14.

Noll, R. (1974a), 'Alternatives in Sports Policy', in R. Noll (ed.), *Government and the Sport Business*, Washington, DC: The Brookings Institution, pp. 411–28.

Noll, R. (1974b), 'Attendance and Price Setting', in R. Noll (ed.), *Government and the Sport Business*, Washington, DC: The Brookings Institution, pp. 115–58.

Noll, R. (ed.) (1974c), *Government and the Sport Business*, Washington, DC: The Brookings Institution.

Noll, R. (1999), 'Competition Policy in European Sports after the Bosman Case', in C. Jeanrenaud and S. Késenne (eds), *Competition Policy in Professional Sports*, Antwerp: Standaard Editions Ltd.

Noll, R. (2002), 'The Economics of Promotion and Relegation in Sports Leagues: The Case of English Football', *Journal of Sports Economics*, 3 (2), 169–203.

Noll, R. (2003), 'The Economics of Baseball Contraction', *Journal of Sports Economics*, 4 (4), 367–88.

Provost, P. (2003a), *Revenue Sharing and Level of Talent in the League*, Discussion paper, Université Libre de Bruxelles.

Provost, P. (2003b), *Peculiarity of Professional Sports Teams in Europe: The International Transfers*, Discussion paper, Université Libre de Bruxelles.

Quirk, J. and M. El-Hodiri (1974), 'The Economic Theory of a Professional League', in R. Noll (ed.), *Government and the Sport Business*, Washington, DC: Brookings Institution, pp. 33–80.

Quirk, J. and R. Fort (1992), *Pay Dirt: The Business of Professional Team Sports*, Princeton: Princeton University Press.

Quirk, J. and R. Fort (1999), *Hard Ball: The Abuse of Power in Pro Team Sports*, Princeton: Princeton University Press.

Rascher, D. (1997), 'A Model of a Professional Sports League', in W. Hendricks (ed.), *Advances in the Economics of Sport*, Vol. 2, Greenwich and London: JAI Press, pp. 27–76.

Rosen, S. (1981), 'The Economics of Superstars', *American Economic Review*, 71 (4), 845–98.

Ross, S. (1991), 'Break Up the Sports League Monopolies', in P. Staudohar and J. Mangan (eds), *The Business of Professional Sports*, Urbana: University of Illinois Press.

Rottenberg, S. (1956), 'The Baseball Players' Labor Market', *Journal of Political Economy*, 64 (3), 242–58.

Sanderson, A. (2002), 'The Many Dimensions of Competitive Balance', *Journal of Sports Economics*, 3 (2), 204–28.

Sandy, R., P. Sloane and M. Rosentraub (2004), *The Economics of Sport: An International Perspective*, New York: Palgrave Macmillan.

Scully, G. (1974), 'Pay and Performance in Major League Baseball', *American Economic Review*, 64 (6), 915–30.

Scully, G. (1989), *The Business of Major League Baseball*, Chicago: University of Chicago Press.

Scully, G. (ed.) (1992), *Advances in the Economics of Sport*, Vol. 1, Greenwich: JAI Press.

Scully, G. (1995), *The Market Structure of Sports*, Chicago: University of Chicago Press.

Scully, G. (1999), 'Free Agency and the Rate of Monopsonistic Exploitation in Baseball', in C. Jeanrenaud and S. Késenne (eds), *Competition Policy in Professional Sports*, Antwerp: Standaard Editions Ltd.

Siegfried, J. and C. Hinshaw (1979), 'The Effects of Lifting TV Blackouts on Professional Football No-shows', *Journal of Economics and Business*, 32 (1), 1–13.

Simmons, R. and B. Buraimo (2005), *Television Viewing and Stadium Attendance: Cannibalization or Complements?*, Working paper, Lancaster University, UK.

Sloane, P. (1969), 'The Labour Market in Professional Football', *British Journal of Industrial Relations*, 7 (2), 181–99.

Sloane, P. (1971), 'The Economics of Professional Football: The Football Club as a Utility Maximiser', *Scottish Journal of Political Economy*, 17 (2), 121–46.

Sloane, P. (1980), *Sport in the Market?* Hobart Paper No 85, London: Institute of Economic Affairs.

Solow, R. (1979), 'Another Possible Source of Wage Stickiness', *Journal of Macroeconomics*, 1 (1), 79–82.

Sommers, P. (1992), *Diamonds are Forever: The Business of Baseball*, Washington, DC: The Brookings Institution.

Staudohar, P. (1999), 'Labor Relations in Basketball: The Lockout of 1998–99', *Monthly Labor Review*, US Department of Labor, April, 3–9.

Staudohar, P. and J. Mangan (eds) (1991), *The Business of Professional Sports*, Urbana and Chicago: University of Illinois Press.

Szymanski, S. (2001), 'Income Inequality, Competitive Balance and Attractiveness of Team Sports: Some Evidence and a Natural Experiment from English Soccer', *Economic Journal*, III (469), F4–F26.

Szymanski, S. (2003), 'The Economic Design of Sporting Contests', *Journal of Economic Literature*, 41 (4), 1137–87.

Szymanski S. (2004), 'Professional Team Sports are a Game: The Walrasian Fixed-Supply Conjecture Model, Contest-Nash Equilibrium, and the Invariance Principle', *Journal of Sports Economics*, 5 (2), 111–26.

Szymanski, S. (2006), 'The Theory of Contests', in J. Fizel (ed.), *Handbook of Sports Economics Research*, London: M.E. Sharpe.

Szymanski, S. and S. Késenne (2004), 'Competitive Balance and Gate Revenue Sharing in Team Sports', *Journal of Industrial Economics*, 51 (4), 513–25.

Szymanski, S. and T. Kuypers (1999), *Winners and Losers: The Business Strategy of Football*, London: Viking.

Szymanski, S. and S. Leach (2005), *Tilting the Playing Field: Why a Sports League Planner Would Choose Less, Not More, Competitive Balance?* Working paper, Tanaka Business School, Imperial College, London.

Van der Burg, T. (1996), 'Het Voetbalmonopolie', *Economisch-Statistische Berichten*, 81 (4070), 710–11.

Van de Burg, T. and A. Prinz (2005), 'Progressive Taxation as a Measure for Improving Competitive Balance', *Scottish Journal of Political Economy*, 52 (1), 65–74.

Vrooman, J. (1995), 'A General Theory of Professional Sports Leagues', *Southern Economic Journal*, 61 (4), 971–90.

Vrooman, J. (1996), 'The Baseball Player's Labor Market Reconsidered', *Southern Economic Journal*, 63 (2), 339–60.

Vrooman, J. (2000), 'The Economics of American Sports Leagues', *Scottish Journal of Political Economy*, 47 (4), 364–98.

Weitzman, M. (1984), *The Share Economy, Conquering Stagflation*, Cambridge, MA: Harvard University Press.

Wiseman, N. (1977), 'The Economics of Football', *Lloyds Bank Review*, 123, 29–43.

Zimbalist, A. (1992), *Baseball and Billions*, New York: Basic Books.

Zimbalist, A. (ed.) (2001), *The Economics of Sport*, Vols 1 and 2, Cheltenham, UK and Northampton, MA, US: Edward Elgar.

Zimbalist, A. (2003), 'Sport as Business', *Oxford Review of Economic Policy*, 19 (4), 503–11.

Index